ADULT
ILLITERACY IN
THE
UNITED STATES

ADULT
ILLITERACY IN
THE
UNITED STATES

A Report to the
Ford Foundation

By
Carman St. John Hunter
World Education

with
David Harman
Hebrew University

McGRAW-HILL BOOK COMPANY
New York   St. Louis   San Francisco
Auckland   Bogotá   Düsseldorf   Johannesburg   London   Madrid
Mexico   Montreal   New Delhi   Panama   Paris   São Paulo
Singapore   Sydney   Tokyo   Toronto

Thomas Quinn and Michael Hennelly were the editors of this
book. The designer was Elaine Gongora. Sally Fliess super-
vised the production. This book was set in Times Roman by
Offset Composition Services, Inc., and it was printed and
bound by R. R. Donnelley and Sons.

Library of Congress Cataloging in Publication Data
Hunter, Carman St. John.
  Adult illiteracy in the United States.

  Bibliography: p.
  Includes index.
  1. Illiteracy—United States. I. Harman,
David, joint author. II. Ford Foundation.
III. Title.
  LC151.H86   374' .012   79-1020
  ISBN 0-07-031380-6

1 2 3 4 5 6 7 8 9 RRD RRD 7 9 8 0 3 2 1 0 9

Contents

༄

FIGURES

TABLES

Foreword

〇〇

How people learn is a subject of endless fascination. Scholars from various disciplines and many countries have long explored the subject with enormous energy. In recent years the federal government of the United States has underwritten an extensive amount and range of research about learning. The Ford Foundation, among other private organizations, has also supported a variety of efforts—including work by Swiss psychologist Jean Piaget and his collaborators, research on curriculum design and student learning assessment at the British Open University, studies at Rockefeller University on how individuals from different ethnic groups and cultural backgrounds develop and apply learning skills, and reassessment by American scholars of theories of achievement testing.

But despite the wealth of research on learning, it became evident by the mid-1970s that there is only a weak connection between basic learning research and its actual application in schools, postsecondary institutions, and other educational settings. In response to this problem, the Ford Foundation embarked with the approval of its Board of Trustees on a modest program of grants and projects to advance understanding and use of the processes and findings of learning research.

To help guide the development of our program, since 1975 we have been conducting an in-house seminar on learning to keep the staff informed about what is going on in learning research and the extent to which the results of that work, where appropriate, are being understood and incorporated into educational planning, policy development, and practice throughout the country. In this context, we have occasionally invited scholars and practitioners to present papers on discrete topics and problems. We have also commissioned a few in-depth reports on broad, multi-dimensional issues that sometimes have implications well beyond the field of learning theory and application itself. Some of the products have seemed to us to deserve a wider audience and we have taken steps to have them published and made available publicly.

One of these is a report by David Wiley and Annegret Harnischfeger of CEMREL, Inc. which analyzes the decline in test scores in the United States.[1] Another is a paper by Donald H. Graves of the University of New Hampshire on learning to write and the teaching of writing in the schools.[2] This report on adult illiteracy in the United States, by Carman St. John Hunter of World Education and David Harman of the Hebrew University of Jerusalem and Harvard, is still another. The thinking which led to it, and the particular context in which it was carried out, account in large part for its shape and character.

The level of literacy of adults in the United States is a matter that has sometimes been overshadowed by our nation's concerns with the schooling of its young. Surveys addressed to the subject have come and gone, having little impact in a country that prides itself on its educational programs, its information systems, and its relatively high rate of literacy. Programs to provide literacy training for adults abound, and many of them are quite good. Yet it has become increasingly clear that these reach only a small fraction of adults in need of basic literacy skills. Is it that the nation simply needs to pump more money into expanding and spreading programs that already exist? Is it that we need to develop radically different instructional and delivery approaches? Or is the solution, perhaps, somewhere in between? Can we even begin to answer these questions without rethinking our definitions of literacy and our ideas about what "basic" literacy skills are? Can we do *this* without understanding more about adult illiterates themselves—not just how they learn, but who they are, why there are so many, what their life circumstances and problems are, what *they* think they need? These were some of the broad questions and concerns underlying the Foundation's decision to commission a report on the subject of adult illiteracy in the United States.

---

[1]David Wiley and Annegret Harnischfeger, *Achievement Test Score Decline: Do We Need to Worry?*, CEMREL, Inc., 1976. (Copies available from CEMREL, Inc., 3120 59th Street, St. Louis, Missouri 63139.)

[2]Donald H. Graves, "Balance the Basics: Let Them Write—A Report to the Ford Foundation," Ford Foundation, 1978. (Copies available from the Ford Foundation, P.O. Box 559, Naugatuck, Connecticut 06770.)

Our desire to examine the subject led us in 1975 into conversations with the president and staff of World Education who, by an accident of timing, had approached us to discuss their experiences and concerns about the field. The organization is known primarily for its many years of pioneering work in nonformal education and functional literacy in developing countries. But in 1972, at UNESCO's Third International Conference on Adult Education in Tokyo, World Education sponsored a spirited, day-long workshop in which a prominent Thai official with whom they were working reported on new approaches in adult learning and the success they were achieving in his land. American adult educators and government officials present at that session were so impressed that they encouraged World Education to think about the applicability of their international experience to the literacy problems of adult learners in the United States.

With government funding, World Education subsequently mounted a series of experiments in adult basic education in eight states. As was the case in their work with the developing countries, their emphasis in these programs was on helping teachers and learners to assess their own needs and to develop their own learning materials. They found, as they expected, that the self-defined concerns, needs, and objectives of the participants were similar to those they had encountered in the developing countries. But they found themselves struggling with two aspects of the U.S. adult literacy problem which seemed quite culture specific. One was that those adults who enroll in American literacy programs are largely self-selected and therefore not representative of the nation's "functionally illiterate" population. The second was that it is extremely difficult to assess and address the problems of adult illiteracy in a nation where schooling is both available and compulsory and where the magnitude of the problem is not widely appreciated.

On the basis of our discussions with World Education staff, our knowledge of their wide-ranging experience in adult literacy, and consultation with outside advisors, in late 1976 we asked the organization to undertake a study for us on adult illiteracy in the United States. This report, in which Carman St. John Hunter and David Harman came to play the key roles, is the result of that study. Its preparation has been a major undertaking, requiring the cooperation and involvement of many people over a period of nearly two years. Its publication comes at a time when the problems of adult illiteracy appear to be reemerging in the national consciousness.

As readers will find, the report covers a great deal of ground. It discusses definitions and labels, and the conceptual underpinning that has led to their use and their usefulness. It gathers and analyzes data on which and how many adults need help with literacy. It attempts to characterize these adults in ways that will foster a deeper understanding of them and make it clearer why planners, policy-makers, and practitioners need to care about them. It explores a wide range of efforts, both formal and nonformal, that are designed to advance adult literacy, and it gives us a glimpse of what is known and not known about the effectiveness of such efforts. Perhaps most important, it puts adult illiteracy as an educational problem into the larger context of our changing society and makes some particularly cogent observations and recommendations. For those who wish to dig deeper into the subject, an annotated bibliography has been provided.

We believe the report to be an important addition to our series on learning. It offers a fresh perspective and a new way of thinking about the phenomenon of adult illiteracy. It is large in vision and deep in sensitivity. Whether or not there is unanimous agreement on its viewpoint, we think that its readers will find it instructive and challenging in their efforts to deal with the huge and difficult problem of adult illiteracy in the United States, and perhaps, elsewhere.

Edward J. Meade, Jr.
Ford Foundation
April 1979

ADULT ILLITERACY IN THE UNITED STATES

PROLOGUE

༼

Why Should We Care About Adult Illiteracy?

Americans have recently been confronted and confounded by dramatic headlines about the level of illiteracy among the adult population. The *New York Times* of April 24, 1977, declared: "Illiteracy of Adults Called U.S. Disease." Other stories made equally disturbing claims, including that one adult in five does not possess the functional competency to get along in this society. The increasing visibility of this issue prompted conversations between World Education and the Ford Foundation and led to the Foundation's request to World Education for a basic information paper on the subject.

Much of our perspective on illiteracy in the United States has grown from insights gained from studying World Education's experience both in this country and in many parts of the developing world. Founded in 1951, World Education is a private, nonprofit organization that provides training in the technical skills needed to develop and carry out programs in nonformal education.[1] World Education began with a clear focus on functional literacy training in India, but discovered, as its work spread to over 20 countries in Asia, Africa, and Latin America, that illiterate adults rarely perceive literacy per se as a solution to the immediate problems they face in their daily lives. World Education has therefore shifted its central focus over the years to

---

[1] *Nonformal education* is generally defined as "any organized educational activity outside the established formal system—whether operating separately or as an important feature of some broader activity—that is intended to serve identifiable learning clienteles and learning objectives" (Coombs, 1973, p. 11).

1

a more integrated educational approach embracing all aspects of individual and community development. Helping people to acquire conventional literacy skills has become only one part of a far wider objective.[2]

Initial work on the paper led us to educational agencies for data. Statistics from the U.S. Office of Education of the Department of Health, Education, and Welfare (HEW) and from the National Advisory Council on Adult Education (NACAE) revealed the progress made by federally assisted state programs to create opportunities for educationally disadvantaged adults. (The term *educationally disadvantaged adults* refers to persons 16 years and older who are not enrolled in school and who have not completed secondary school.) The data revealed not only progress made, but also an incredible gap between the numbers of persons who might be seen as needing such assistance and those who were actually receiving it—whether through the new programs or through any alternative means.

Many goverment reports have noted the difficulties in coordinating basic education programs with other federal programs for adults and even with other Office of Education programs. When administrative responsibility was shifted to the states, even minimal coordination simply did not occur. One report pointed out that "both the adult basic education and the antipoverty programs, as well as other state and local programs, are designed to serve essentially the same population—the disadvantaged" (*The Adult Basic Education Program*, 1975, p. 18).

We found another gap between the stated objectives of most educational programs for the disadvantaged and any reasonable possibility that such objectives could be fulfilled by education alone. For us, this raised fundamental questions about some of the assumptions of our society. What is education for? Who and what determine who shall be educated? How is the educational system connected with and influenced by other institutions in the society? We realized anew how directly the level of program funding reflects the perceived importance—and power—of the people for whom a program is designed.

Education, perhaps more than any other institution or function

---

[2]*Conventional literacy* is the ability to read, write, and comprehend texts on familiar subjects and to understand whatever signs, labels, instructions, and directions are necessary to get along within one's environment. A detailed discussion of other kinds of literacy and the whole problem of definitions follows in Chapter One.

of society, mirrors the basic presuppositions and values of that society, whether these are stated openly or implied through social mechanisms. We were thrust inevitably into a dialogue about education and development. Does lack of education produce poverty, or does poverty produce educational disadvantage? What is human development? Can it be furthered by industry, technology, and the scientific view of reality, or is something missing in that construct? In what ways and to what degree is education used as a means of social control and pacification?

We kept these questions in mind as we read the literature and talked with the experts. Our work on this study has been something like an archaeological expedition: successive digs, each uncovering new layers of materials and insights. We have searched out published and unpublished materials. Everything we have used is available to those who have the time and interest to pursue it. Ours is not a technical report, but rather an overview of what is known about adult illiteracy in the United States and some of the issues that condition raises. The annotated bibliography in Appendix C should assist both those who wish to explore some of the literature about adult illiteracy and those who seek more detailed information about specific aspects of the problem.

We hope that the report will stimulate public consideration of these issues and assist educators and those outside educational circles who are deeply interested in public policy in this area.

What we found in the course of this study has confirmed our previous experience. Just as the problems faced by people everywhere are interrelated, so too must be the efforts to solve them. This study looks at adult education as an integral part of the larger social and economic system. We believe that schools, adult education programs, and the total system of formal and nonformal education for all ages reflect our society's vision of itself and its goals.

We are part of a world in which economic and social disparities between advantaged and disadvantaged persons, groups, and nations remain unresolved by technology. Nor has material progress resolved questions of human value and purpose. Indeed, industrial growth has itself threatened the environment and life-support systems. Moreover, large, transnational corporations have independent power to decide the future of whole peoples without their participation in any determination of social priorities. National and state governments are far removed from local concerns. "One person, one vote" has become a concept that for many seems to bear little relation to their power to affect what happens to them and the communities in which they live.

Our national response to these conditions will determine who receives what kind of education in the future. Do we see education solely as a way to provide the labor force with sufficient skills and information to continue to move us in the direction we are going? Or are there, perhaps, new patterns of education and work that will build in people other qualities and skills for living full lives? How is the potential for resolving social and personal problems nurtured in our society?

Some may see these questions as too amorphous to be taken seriously in a study of adult illiteracy. It is our conviction that a mere rearrangement of educational furniture is too simplistic an approach to the resolution of the social and economic issues of which illiteracy is only a symptom. For too long we have tried to make literacy the answer to more serious national and international problems. Educators have, on the one hand, claimed too much for education and, on the other, have dissociated themselves from responsibility for social questions. We believe that the interconnectedness between policy decisions and assumptions in the field of education and in other areas that affect the total life of a people call for new alliances and an integration of insights from different disciplines and from diverse segments of the population.

Neither we nor those whose analyses have influenced us possess blueprints for the future. Brazilian educator Paulo Freire's conviction that all persons must become active participants in analyzing their world and in changing the conditions of their lives seems to us to apply particularly to citizens who feel powerless (Freire, 1970). In his work with Syracuse University's Civic Literacy Project, Warren Ziegler (1977) expresses a concern for "human agency," that is, the participation of the total population in the modification of social experience. As a leading proponent of nonformal adult education, Lyra Srinivasan's goal of releasing the hidden potential within each person—creativity, confidence, resourcefulness, a willingness to take chances—suggests that all members of society can contribute to the amelioration of harmful conditions (Srinivasan, 1977b). We concur with all three that this is what education is about.

In this study, we examine data in three different areas:

1. Changing concepts of literacy and illiteracy and the interaction between the demands placed on persons in an

increasingly complex society and their aspirations in that society

2. The groups within U.S. society for whom present educational arrangements have been least effective—that is, those groups in which the largest number of persons with literacy difficulties are found

3. The programs and services offered to adults who seek to remedy deficiencies in their earlier education

Our conclusions and recommendations focus on new ways of reaching those most in need and on involving citizens and policy makers in addressing the basic social issues that ultimately affect education at every level.

Many individuals and organizations helped us in our study. We acknowledge our debts to them in Appendix B, which also lists persons we consulted in the preparation of this report.

CHAPTER
ONE

∽

What Is Adult Illiteracy?

Alarmed by recent statements in the media that large numbers of adult Americans are "illiterate" or "functionally illiterate," educators and the public have begun to ask what an acceptable standard of literacy should be for an adult American in the last half of the 20th century. Our study leads us to believe that all definitions of literacy or illiteracy are completely relative. We tie the terms, therefore, to social aspirations and functional criteria. Our definitions place the burden of describing levels and needed skills on the individuals concerned and on the social groups to which they belong. Within the general term *literacy*, we suggest the following distinctions:

1. *Conventional literacy*: the ability to read, write, and comprehend texts on familiar subjects and to understand whatever signs, labels, instructions, and directions are necessary to get along within one's environment.

2. *Functional literacy*: the possession of skills *perceived as necessary by particular persons and groups* to fulfill their own self-determined objectives as family and community members, citizens, consumers, job-holders, and members of social, religious, or other associations of their choosing. This includes the ability to obtain information they want and to use that information for their own and others' well-being; the ability to read and write adequately to satisfy the requirements *they set for themselves* as being important for their own lives; the ability to deal positively with demands made on them by society;

and the ability to solve the problems they face in their daily lives.

What is the extent of adult illiteracy—conventional and functional—in the United States? Who is affected? What is being done about it? By whom? What more is required? How can it be accomplished? At what cost? These questions seemed to be a logical basis for this study. Our early uneasiness about the simplicity of this approach, however, was soon translated into significant difficulties.

Experience in other countries suggests that literacy is seldom a first priority among those who are themselves unlettered. When given an opportunity to define their own needs, they are likely to stress first their economic problems, followed by such personal concerns as family living, child care, health, and nutrition. What bearing, if any, does this have on adult life in the United States? Furthermore, if fewer than 2 million adults are enrolled in current programs designed—as the figures suggest—to meet the needs of 60 million, is it possible that the programs themselves are defective? What else is responsible for the enormous gap between the population whose education is in some sense deficient and those benefiting from current programs?

We discovered among those concerned with adult illiteracy four different ways of understanding its causes and four related approaches to its solution.

1. Some concentrate on what they see as the failure of *the schools* and see educational reforms within the schools as the key to decreasing adult illiteracy.
2. Others see a need for change within the field of *adult education* and address themselves to improving teaching methods in programs of special or basic education for individuals and groups with literacy difficulties.
3. A third approach concentrates on the *educational system*, seeing in the concept of life-long learning a potential to respond to the needs of all ages and all segments of the population, including adults with low levels of educational achievement.
4. A fourth approach, with which we concur, sees each of the above as too limited to address fully the root causes of adult illiteracy and suggests that only a radical rethinking of the purposes and patterns of education as a function of the larger *social system* can achieve long-range changes. In this view, education mirrors and per-

petuates the social and economic ills of the society as a whole and depends on society's goals for its direction.

These approaches to meeting the needs of adults with low levels of educational attainment are not mutually exclusive, but their emphases are different. For each approach Table 1 identifies the major concerns, areas of deficiency, goals, and means to attain those goals.

This study is about adult illiteracy in the United States. While we believe that school reform and such concepts as life-long education are relevant and perhaps even essential, our attention in this report is directed toward the areas that seem to us to promise the most immediate help for those 16 years and over who are not in school and whose educational attainment is so limited as to constitute a serious difficulty for them. At the same time, we must address the underlying causes of their present situation and seek solutions that will make a difference to future generations. We therefore place priority on those educational programs that are immediately helpful to illiterate adults and on the larger social issues that affect not only current adult education programs, but also the schools and the consideration of learning as a life-long undertaking.

High-quality programs, readily accessible to those who seek them, are an urgent need that cannot be overlooked even as we search for long-range strategies. Many adults now overcome embarrassment to enter tutoring programs and basic education classes. They expend precious time and energy to seek credentials. Some pursue job-related skills or information to help them as community members or parents. We shall look at what exists to meet their needs and search for new approaches that may improve the quality of what is offered with the hope also of serving those who are not now being reached.

For all those who enroll in present programs there are many more whose entrapment in poverty make even conventional literacy a low priority for them. Research suggests that poverty and the power structures of society are more responsible for low levels of literacy than the reverse (Bazany, et al., 1970a, 1970b; Bazany, 1973; Blaug, 1966, p. 400; Harman, 1974, chap. 2; Lerner, 1958, pp. 54–61). For most persons who lack literacy skills, illiteracy is simply one factor interacting with many others— class, race and sex discrimination, welfare dependency, unemployment, poor housing, and a general sense of powerlessness. The acquisition of reading and writing skills would eliminate

TABLE 1
Four Approaches To Adult Illiteracy

	SCHOOLS	ADULT EDUCATION	EDUCATIONAL SYSTEM	SOCIAL SYSTEM
MAJOR CONCERNS	Why are reading levels so low? Why do high school graduates so often fail to meet expected standards? How can we attain quality given rising costs and tighter budgets? What can we do about the deterioration of urban schools and its consequences for the learning of the children of the poor? (These questions are infinite in range and number, and represent enormous public and professional dissatisfaction with schools and recent reforms.)	How can we reach and motivate those who lack basic or functional literacy? Are their learning needs and styles different from other adults? How can we retain them once enrolled? How do they move from initial tutoring to more advanced work? How can what we know about adult learning be applied to disadvantaged adults? Who are the best teachers? What training do they need? How do innovations in methods spread? Can we use mass media for this purpose? For motivating potential students? For instruction?	Do certain skills and knowledge *have* to be acquired at specific times and places in the life cycle? Can education be understood as a life-long, recurrent process, with persons alternating between periods of work and study? Can those who had not acquired literacy skills in their early years do so easily and without stigma as adults? How can people set their own learning objectives and progress at their own speed?	What are the prevailing assumptions and values of our society? How do these affect the learning of adults with multiple disadvantages—the poor, unemployed, victims of ethnic or racial discrimination? What is the relationship between the educational structures and the structures of power in economic and political life? What is the relation between education and work? How does society view itself in relation to the interests of all the racial and ethnic subgroups within its own body? In relation to the global community?

NATURE OF THE "DEFICIT"	Current school practice and programs make it difficult or impossible for certain children to learn.	Present programs and delivery systems are inadequate to meet the needs of adults with educational deficiencies.	Narrow concepts and presuppositions limit the opportunities provided for education.	Social and economic structures of dominance, perpetuated in the schools make it hard for many to learn.
GOAL	To enable those who fail in school to learn within the educational system.	To help adults with educational deficiencies to become contributing members of the mainstream society.	To make available "appropriate opportunities for life-long learning without regard to restrictions of previous education or training, . . . social or ethnic background, or economic circumstances" (Public Law 94-482).	To develop economic structures that are more responsive to human values and forms of governance and work that are more democratic and participatory.
MEANS FOR CHANGE	A variety of special or remedial programs, including, at present, "back to basics."	More programs; better programs and methods to make basic education more attractive and more effective; a more effective delivery system, making it easier for disadvantaged persons to benefit.	The marshalling of all learning resources, public and private, to guarantee that every community is able to supply the needs of its members.	Direct participation by the poor and others generally excluded from decision-making in the construction of solutions to major problems, including educational.

conventional illiteracy among many but would have no appreciable effect on the other factors that perpetuate the poverty of their lives.

We earlier asserted that all definitions of literacy or illiteracy, including ours, are relative to time and place. It behooves us to justify that assertion by looking in more detail at how expectations and standards in particular societies at specific times affect definitions of literacy, at some of the problems of measuring literacy levels that flow therefrom, and at the interplay between cultural and economic factors on the one hand and concepts of literacy on the other.

Chapter II tries to answer the question about who the adult illiterates in American society are. Chapter III describes current educational programs and services, and Chapter IV sets forth our conclusions and the recommendations that flow from them. First, however, it is essential to get a grip on the elusive ambiguities of literacy and how it is inextricably embedded in its social and cultural settings. One person's illiteracy may be another's quite satisfactory way of life; your comfortably literate life-style may rest squarely on my educational disadvantages; and what was a quite acceptable standard of literacy in New York in 1850 may be far less useful in Manhattan in 1979.

EXPECTATIONS AND STANDARDS

Concern by governments and international agencies about levels of literacy in the general population is a 20th century phenomenon, particularly intense after World War II and the founding of the United Nations. Not until the 1950s were any systematic worldwide statistics on literacy gathered. There is still no uniformly accepted definition of the rudimentary characteristics of adult literacy. Despite several proposals for international yardsticks, countries—and even areas within countries—employ different measures of literacy. We shall briefly examine the definitional dilemma as it has developed in the United States and around the world since World War II.

Two different sets of expectations affect literacy standards within any society. On the one hand, a society has expectations about the *quality* or *level* of literacy required or desirable for its members and, on the other, it has expectations about the *percentage* of the population that actually meets that standard or may reasonably be expected to do so at some future date. Societies vary greatly with respect to both of these expectations (Resnick and Resnick, 1977).

When the simplest, most rudimentary definitions of literacy are applied to industrialized countries, a high level of literacy can be claimed for the majority of their populations, despite the sometimes startlingly sizable subgroups of nonreaders in print-oriented cultures. Most people use the term *literacy* in one of its most fundamental senses: the ability to read and to write one's name; or the 1951 UNESCO definition: "A person is literate who can with understanding both read and write a short, simple statement on his everyday life" (*Literacy as a Factor in Development*, 1965). The level of expectation in these definitions is obviously low. In the United States, the majority of the population is able to fulfill it to a degree that is unprecedented.

It may come as a surprise to learn, however, that not until the 1920s was any higher expectation held for the general public in this country. Although the ideals proclaimed for the growing public school system have always been broad, the high drop-out rates and selective promotions screened out a far larger proportion of the population than is true today, when we are beginning to see this screening as a national problem. It has become a problem partly because our expectations about the quality of education and the numbers of persons who should be educated have risen considerably.

Early efforts to achieve mass literacy in Western Europe and in the United States were carried out by religious bodies. Their goal was less to teach reading for understanding than to promote fluency in the oral reading of familiar biblical and liturgical texts. This continued to be the primary goal in the 17th and early 18th century public schools. With the gradual secularization of public education, civic and national subject matter replaced religious texts but the goals and methods did not change substantially. Homely virtues, acculturation, and the history of the nation were taught. Reading skills continued to be based on accurate and fluent pronunciation in oral exercises (Resnick and Resnick, 1977).

Testing procedures developed for use with Army recruits in World War I revealed the reading difficulties of soldiers and gave impetus to the expansion of testing, now an integral part of the American educational system. The ability to read and answer questions became more important than skill at simply declaiming familiar material. Changes in instruction resulted and the groundwork was laid for higher expectations about the appropriate quality of literacy in schools for the masses. This change, coupled with the gradually increasing numbers of persons who remained longer in the public schools, raised the level of literacy expectations for the general population.

In many nations newly independent after World War II adult literacy became a high national priority. New governments sought to include vast numbers of unschooled people in economic and social development. Early in the history of worldwide conferences on literacy, attempts to define literacy in an international arena, where expectations and experience varied so widely, resulted in broad definitions that focused more on the *functions* of literacy than on specific standards or content.

> A person is functionally literate when he has acquired the knowledge and skills in reading and writing which enable him to engage effectively in all those activities in which literacy is normally assumed in his cultural group.
>
> —proposed by William Gray,
1956, and included in the
Encyclopedia of Education

In 1962, UNESCO stated that:

> A person is literate when he has acquired the essential knowledge and skills which enable him to engage in all those activities in which literacy is required for effective functioning in his group and community and whose attainments in reading, writing, and arithmetic make it possible for him to continue to use these skills toward his own and the community's development.

The concept of functional literacy was, perhaps, a natural outgrowth of liberal social thought, an attempt to state that persons and societies need more than reading and writing skills. Many definitions linked personal pride and dignity to being able to support oneself and one's family, to a sense of direction in life, and to creative participation in community- and nation-building.

The unfortunate tendency to use terms like *literacy* and *functional literacy* loosely and interchangeably has led to many misapprehensions and unfounded claims, especially with reference to the term *development*. Resulting confusions and controversies that have seriously affected attitudes toward literacy and clear communication about literacy goals include:

1. The assertion that economic development, increased gross national product, and modernization automatically follow or are contingent upon literacy.

2. The parallel claim that *anyone* who becomes literate is automatically better off economically, is better able to find employment, and becomes a better citizen.[3]
3. The claim, even after narrow economic goals were decried as too utilitarian and limiting, that literacy might somehow bring about national development in the broadest sense of the term.
4. The equating of illiteracy with inferiority, backwardness, cultural poverty, and low intelligence.
5. The disregard for what individuals and groups themselves need and want within their own social settings and the imposition of programs believed to be "good" for them.

These oversimplified assumptions about literacy have given rise to a long series of unsuccessful literacy campaigns. Promoters of literacy so zealously stated some of these claims that they raised hopes that have never been fulfilled. Any challenge was heard as denial of the value of literacy. The confusion has caused positions to be frozen.

The long association between development and literacy suggests that we need to clarify our use of the former term as well as to provide workable definitions of literacy and functional literacy. We prefer a broad definition of development that embraces humanistic goals and is not limited to economic stability. Justice and freedom from whatever forces oppress or inhibit self-determination are included in our understanding of both individual and national development.

The argument for definitions that are broader than those implied in the simple literacy–economic development equation rests on the lack of any evidence that literacy per se contributes significantly to wider employment opportunities. Basic education students rarely attribute a new job to increased literacy skills (Greenleigh Associates, 1968; Patten and Clark, 1968). And if it is true, as mounting evidence suggests, that literacy skills are not sought unless they are generally considered desirable within the culture—that is, unless "literacy consciousness" is the norm

---

[3]This claim undergirded the federal legislation in the United States authorizing the Adult Basic Education [ABE] program. Literacy, it was claimed, would help those with low-level literacy skills "to eliminate their inability to get or retain employment," would make them "less likely to become dependent on others," and would increase "their ability to benefit from occupational training" [Title III of Public Law 91-230, Amendment to the Adult Education Act, Section 303c].

(Bazany et al., 1970b)—then it is probable that literacy skills follow rather than precede development.[4]

MEASURING LITERACY LEVELS

In the United States major changes in expectations about levels of literacy and its extension within the population have followed periods of war. We noted the extension of teaching for the understanding of written material in the 1920s. During World War II, the U.S. Army discovered for the second time in our national experience that draftees did not meet the expectations of those responsible for their training. They were again found to lack the ability to understand military tasks on the basis of written instructions. As a result, a new effort was made to describe the dimensions of the "literacy problem" in objective, quantifiable terms.

The most immediately accessible measure was grade-level equivalency. The Army selected fifth grade as a convenient standard for literacy. Research studies have consistently thrown into question the validity of standard testing procedures and grade-level criteria for describing either the intelligence or the cognitive skills of children, but, at the time, no other procedures were available. The application of such arbitrary criteria to adults is even more questionable. It is also obvious that the number of school years completed at some time in the past does not define the level of proficiency obtained at that time, nor does it in any way guarantee retention in adult life.[5]

---

[4]The persistence of the literacy-brings-development theme was evident in UNESCO's Experimental World Literacy Program. The design itself did not provide any means for testing other hypotheses. There are many references in the assessment report to the necessity for including the political, economic, cultural, and social dimensions of experience in educational programs and on seeing literacy as but one element in life-long education. However, the appendix to the assessment, which sets forth the "Recommendations of the Expert Team on Evaluation of Experimental Literacy Projects," concludes not with a call for radical change in these areas, but once again with a call for literacy, which it claims is essential to raise cultural levels, "to break with a past of ignorance linked to domination and exploitation . . . to build a democratic society, and as a duty of international solidarity in the perspective of a new world aborning" (*Experimental World Library Programs: A Critical Assessment*, 1976, p. 191).

[5]The choice of the fifth grade level as an international criterion for functional literacy is related to a study done in the Philippines by Flores (1950) showing that, to retain a level of functional literacy (in Tagalog) 15 years after leaving school, at least four or five years of primary schooling are required. Although

As functional literacy became a more commonly accepted standard, the problem of objective measurement increased. What was to be measured? Studies by Louis Harris and Associates (1970 and 1971) attempted to determine the abilities of Americans to use such written materials as bus schedules, employment ads, telephone dialing instructions, and application forms. In the military, Project REALISTIC concentrated on the degree to which low literacy levels could interfere with job performance (Sticht, Caylor, Kern, and Fox, 1972).

While some advocates of the functional literacy concept settled, at least temporarily, for the conclusion that "the standard of attainment in functional literacy may be equated to the skills in reading, writing and arithmetic achieved after a set number of years of primary or elementary schooling" (UNESCO, 1962), the search for a way to define and test desired adult levels of competency went on. A new direction originated in 1970 from the Conference on Strategies for Generating a Nationwide Adult Right-to-Read Effort. The challenge, they said, was "to foster through every means the ability to read, write, and compute with functional competence needed for meeting the requirements of adult living" (*Report of the North Carolina Conference*, 1970).

On the basis of this definition, the Division of Adult Education of the Office of Education undertook in 1971 to sponsor a study intended to identify the competencies needed by an adult American. The study, which involved no grade-level equivalencies, was originally called *adult performance level* (or APL, by which it is still commonly known) and later *adult functional competence*. Its findings are presented in a report called "Adult Functional Competency: A Report to the Office of Education Dissemination Review Panel" published in 1975 by the Division of Extension of the University of Texas at Austin, which carried out the project.

APL research defined some 65 objectives—requirements for adult living—keyed to five general-knowledge areas. The research team conducted extensive studies and described three levels of functional competency within each category. These

---

the methodological basis of the study has been questioned, Roy and Kapoor's study on literacy retention rates in India also points to four years of schooling as "the critical point at which literacy retention moves from a low to a high level" (Roy and Kapoor, 1975, p. 26). James Sheffield (1977, p. 5), on the other hand, suggests that there is really no specific educational level for permanent retention of literacy and reviews various studies that come to differing conclusions.

levels are associated with different levels of adult success as measured by income, job status, and education. APL 1's are those adults who function with great difficulty; APL 2's are functional in the society but not proficient; APL 3's are those adults who operate with high levels of proficiency (*Adult Functional Competency*, 1975b).

Those who support the basic APL premises claim that they constitute a significant improvement over earlier notions of adult literacy. The criteria for identifying levels of literacy, they maintain, are contained within the definition itself rather than in some external criteria such as grade-level completion. Furthermore, they argue, the criteria are directly related to real tasks within the society rather than to skills generally associated with early schooling.

Critics maintain, on the other hand, that any objectives used as a basis for measurement can be only as accurate and reliable as the judgments of the group that defines them. Objectives constitute "a summation of value-laden opinions," says William Griffith of the University of Chicago (Griffith and Cervero, 1976). Such critics point to the background of the APL-defining group, which was made up largely of academicians, adult basic education administrators and teachers, and a small sample of adults enrolled in basic education classes. Hard-to-reach adults not motivated to seek instruction had no part in defining what *they* understand as necessary competencies for adult life. Others object to the narrow focus of the objectives on success in economic terms and on external, functional skills as opposed to such less-quantifiable objectives as growth in areas that provide personal satisfaction. The excluded objectives include stimulation of imagination, sharpening and extending memory, reflecting on one's place in the world, learning to undertake change in oneself and the world, cultivating skills in interpersonal relations, and expressing creativity. Finally, critics of APL fear that the prompt take-over of the process by commercial firms interested in marketing the tests has not only inhibited continuing correction of the instruments but, through promotion and wide-scale use, has prematurely conferred prestige on concepts and measurements that require additional development (World Education Files).

At present it is possible only to make broad statements about basic or functional literacy levels among American adults. On the assumption that the APL objectives do represent at least some of the competencies needed in our society, we shall look in Chapter II at the findings of the research that has been done. Also, assuming a rough correlation between no or very little schooling and significant difficulties with literacy skills, we shall also analyze the available statistics on grades completed by the adult population. Further, assuming some correlation between functional literacy and income, employment, and racial and ethnic background, we shall examine how these statistics relate to educational achievement.

However, if we take seriously the dynamic interaction between self-defined needs and the requirements of society, measurement of functional literacy becomes infinitely more elusive. Who but the person or group involved can really describe what "effective functioning in one's own cultural group" really means? Who needs to know whether skills can be used "toward personal and community development?" How is a "life of dignity and pride" measured? The basic question may be: Whose needs are served by generalized statistics about the population? We agree with Sylvia Scribner of the National Institute of Education and Michael Cole of Rockefeller University when they conclude, in their studies of the ethnography of literacy among the Vai people of Liberia that, "while attempts to arrive at some overall measures of literacy competencies may be useful for certain comparative purposes, the representation of literacy as a fixed inventory of skills that can be assessed outside of their contexts of application has little utility for educational policies" (Scribner and Cole, 1978, p. 25).

CULTURAL AND ECONOMIC INFLUENCES

Some see education as a multidimensional struggle for domination, economic advantage, and prestige. Sociologist Randall Collins (1977) points out that in the 19th century those at the bottom of the American social and economic heap were led to believe that if they were literate more opportunities would be available to them. As the number of those with educational credentials increased, however, so did the basic requirements for the same level of jobs. Each time competing ethnic minorities reached the educational levels they had been told would lead to economic success and prestige, the game rules were changed. The dominant groups in society, in this case the white middle and upper classes, define job requirements in terms of their own achievements and then impose these as standards for the society as a whole. Collins points to the resulting inflation of educational credentials and suggests that disillusionment is likely among those who purchase such credentials through school attendance when the promised pay-off fails to materialize. The disappointed groups may drop out of the difficult process of schooling.

Warren Ziegler of Syracuse University stresses another aspect of economic reality in his analysis of the literacy/illiteracy question. Those who write papers about, design programs for, and describe the "problem" of illiteracy—educators, social workers, researchers, bureaucrats—do so to meet their own needs. It may well be legitimate, Ziegler concedes, to seek to discover why those with low levels of literacy attend classes. It is equally legitimate, however, to ask teachers, administrators, and policy-makers about *their* motivations. They are, after all, economic beneficiaries—generally with far more at stake than the participants in educational programs. Ivan Illich dramatically states this argument by defining a "problem" as "an imputed lack which turns into more money and power for the problem solver" ("Revolting Development: An Exchange with Ivan Illich," 1977, p. 18).

It is a sociological truism, amply illustrated by changing concepts of literacy, that changes that appear to affect one small part of a society's life may actually set in motion many other, potentially major changes, thus upsetting whatever equilibrium exists. In a study referred to earlier, Resnick and Resnick (1977) argue from historical evidence that if the goal of extending even limited functional literacy to the whole population were consciously adopted, radical changes in pedagogy would be required to accommodate the changes in both the literacy criterion and the target population. If an effort were made to increase the number of persons with higher credentials, then the situation of "inflated credentials" would become even more acute. Collins (1977) hints that such continued "inflation" might provoke a breakdown in the whole educational system. Some see this as a problem of "overeducation": since—except in time of war—there are not enough jobs for all who want to work, many "overqualified" persons take jobs that far less-skilled persons could do, thus forcing the less skilled down or out of the economy. Proponents of this view also see a need for entirely new patterns of work, schooling, and leisure (Best and Stern, 1976).[6]

---

[6]Caroline Persell (1977) suggests the further possibility that higher levels of education for the general population pose radical challenges to the shape of the labor market and how that shape is determined. She contends that the criterion for "overeducation" is a criterion of the labor market and not of the

Changing concepts of adult literacy reflect the changes in all aspects of a society. They may also represent goals that make demands upon existing social, economic, cultural, and political institutions. The goal of universal mass literacy in the 20th century suggests more than mass education; it also suggests mass participation in society's efforts and society's benefits as the context within which literacy skills become functional and necessary.

society as a whole or even of what the persons within it really want. The present disjuncture between people's aspirations and available jobs is not an individual problem of overeducation but is rather the problem of a society whose structure for deciding the direction and extent of growth of the economy is at odds with the expectations of its people for education and the opportunity to use that education in work.

CHAPTER
TWO

Who Are The Adult Illiterates?

The people we are looking at are variously described as illiterate, functionally illiterate, functionally incompetent, educationally disadvantaged, or undereducated. It is unlikely that any of them so describe themselves. They may feel only that they are powerless and at a disadvantage with respect to certain benefits of the society. They may also feel that their ability to achieve personal and work-related goals is limited or nonexistent.

How many such persons are there in the United States? One might assume that the answer to this question is readily available. However, external standards for quantifying literacy or classifying persons in relation to it do not exist. Some facts about conventional literacy are relatively easy to assemble. Persons who have difficulty with basic reading and writing skills are most apt to be found among those who have not completed elementary school. It is also possible to examine statistics about persons who do not have high school diplomas. While all who lack high school diplomas are not functionally illiterate by any means, the evidence is strong that the bulk of those who are functionally illiterate are found among persons who fail to graduate from high school (Fisher, 1978).

Furthermore, in our measurement-loving society, a number of tests have been devised to ascertain the ability of persons to perform a series of basic tasks. These provide rough indications of the number of persons who might fail in such tasks. Whether one can say dogmatically that those with any specific set of

23

difficulties are nonfunctional or functionally illiterate is doubtful. However, like the school-leaving statistics, they may be indicators of particular problems encountered by large numbers of adults in their daily lives.

In the Third World many persons who do not possess even basic literacy skills function effectively in their societies. In the United States and other industrialized nations this is also true for some individuals. Their number will be very small, however, because the demands of complex technological societies reach into every aspect of life.

In this chapter we seek to move closer to an understanding of the lives of the persons represented by the assembled data by relating educational attainment and, to a lesser degree, functional competency to other factors: regional location, urban and rural distribution; poverty, unemployment, and welfare; race, ethnic origin, sex, and age.

The available statistics—however inaccurate, distorted, culturally biased, and occasionally contradictory they may be—do have a kind of gross truth. We invite the reader, therefore, to ponder the figures and their relationships while bearing in mind that, like all numbers, they are single-minded abstractions from complex and changing realities, and thus to a degree inevitably misrepresent the situations they purport to describe.

LIES, DAMNED LIES, AND STATISTICS

The educational planners who gather and publish data disagree not only about what constitutes conventional illiteracy and functional illiteracy but also about who is adult, that is, who should be included in the statistics. Some studies are based on persons over 14 years of age who are out of school; others use 15 as the starting point; still others 16; and some studies begin at age 25. These differences make it difficult to compare statistical reports and to reconcile their implications. Further compounding the confusion, in 1973 the U.S. Bureau of the Census discovered that it had underestimated the total population by about 5,300,000 persons when it counted in 1970. There are also an unknown number of illegal aliens (the Immigration Service puts the figure at a minimum of 850,000)[1] who are not included in the census

---

[1]Other estimates range from 2 million to 20 million. "Most prudent officials first settle on a figure of around 8 million, then qualify it by saying 'give or take

figures, although they may turn up in some of the educational statistics.

Even if we agree on who and how many constitute the adult population, there are, as we noted earlier, no external criteria that definitely indicate conventional or functional literacy. The most widely available statistics come from the census, but the census-taker must rely on what people say about their educational attainment. Those who state that they have completed sixth grade are classified as literate. In the person-to-person sampling, individual census-takers may—or may not—ask those who have not completed sixth grade whether they can "read and write a simple message in any language." In both cases, however, the definitions are left to the census-taker and the respondent.

The available school-leaving statistics do not necessarily correlate with individuals' abilities to function or even to read. Indeed, they may reflect little more than increased age requirements for school attendance. Some cities, for instance, have placed the number of functional illiterates at half the number of their high school graduates. Thirty states have found it necessary to require that those seeking a high school diploma give evidence of being able to read and write at an *eighth grade* level.[2]

In addition to numbers, definitions, and standards of measurement, other confounding factors include bias—whether conscious or unconscious—not only among those who actually record the information, but also among survey-designers, questionnaire-writers, and the publishers of tests designed to measure reading levels or "competency" or coping skills; and the duplication of figures or double reporting that sometimes occurs.

---

5 million.' There is only one solid indication that the population of illegal immigrants is increasing: The sharp rise in the number of them found and expelled by agents of the Immigration and Naturalization Service. In 1966, the service expelled 133,000. Last year, it expelled 793,000" (*The New York Times*, May 1, 1977a).

[2] In 1977 a high-ranking official of the New York City public schools defended the eighth grade reading level as an adequate criterion for high school graduation. He reminded those critical of the school system that most of the young people graduating from New York City high schools had reading levels superior to those of their parents, and pointed out that, by definition, approximately one-half of those graduating from high school will read below twelfth grade level and one-half above.

THE NUMBERS GAME

Despite some discrepancies, two massive sets of data[3] at least suggest the dimensions of functional illiteracy in this country: one deals with "competency levels," the other with school completion.

Using Competency Criteria

The Harris study commissioned by the National Reading Center in 1971 undertook to measure the ability of adult Americans to read and answer questions about a classified newspaper, a telephone directory, and a composite standard application form. From such data as the percentages of the sample unable to answer such questionnaire items as "What is the color of your eyes?" and "How long have you lived at your present address?" the study concluded that some 15 percent of adults have serious reading deficiencies (Harris and Associates, 1971).

It was, however, the 1975 report of the University of Texas at Austin setting forth the findings of its Adult Performance Level (APL) study that first caught the attention of the American media and thus of the public. That study, using sophisticated nationwide sampling techniques, also looked at the adult population from the point of view of individuals' ability to function regardless of their level of academic achievement. The report, citing specific examples and using language that was easily understandable, astonished many people. For example:

> When given a notice posted on a cashier's desk in a store describing the check cashing policy for that store, more than one out of five respondents did not draw the correct conclusion from the notice. . . .
> Fourteen percent of the sample, when asked to fill out a check in a simulated business transaction, made an error so serious that it was unlikely that the check would have cleared the bank (*Adult Functional Competency*, 1975 b, p. 21).

---

[3]This chapter draws on a great many statistical reports and studies. We relied most heavily on the *U.S. Census of the Population: 1970* and on the monthly updates to that census that are published as *Current Population Reports*; on publications of the National Center for Education Statistics (NCES), especially *The Condition of Education: 1976*; the National Advisory Council on Adult Education (NACAE), especially its report dated November 1974, *A Target Population in Adult Education*; the General Accounting Office; and the U.S. Bureau of Labor Statistics.

Thirteen percent of the sample did not address an envelope well enough to insure that it would reach the desired destination, and 24 percent did not place a return address on the same envelope which would insure that it would be returned to the sender if delivery were not possible. These results indicate that an estimated 28 million adults would make a serious error in addressing an envelope (ibid., p. 28).

An official of the U.S. Office of Education, using the competency criteria of the APL study, infers that 57 million Americans do not have skills adequate to perform basic tasks. Almost 23 million Americans lacked the competencies necessary to function in the society (APL category 1). An additional 34 million Americans are able to function, but not proficiently (APL 2's) (Parker, 1976, p. 3). These and similar conclusions were widely reported amidst general cries of alarm.

Using Grade Completion Figures

In the United States, as noted above, completion of secondary school has become a kind of benchmark definition of functional literacy. Adults without high school diplomas are considered disadvantaged, and automatically form the "target population" for adult education activities. This view assumes that those with fewer than 12 years of schooling are less able than high school graduates to attain and sustain employment, earn and gain in earnings, and, in general, to participate fully in adult life. The Adult Education Act, passed by Congress in November 1966, states as its purpose

the establishment of programs of adult public education that will enable all adults to continue their education *to at least the level of completion of secondary school* and make available to them the means to secure training that will enable them to become more employable, productive, and responsible citizens [emphasis added] (Adult Education Act, Section 302, PL 91-230).

It is not surprising, therefore, to discover that most American studies of educational attainment use graduation from twelfth grade as the critical point.

Figure 1 shows the rise in the high school graduation rate since 1870, a rise especially dramatic between 1910 and 1963. In numbers, in percentages, and among almost every segment of the population, more and more Americans are staying in school longer.

FIGURE 1
High School Graduation Rate, 1870–1974

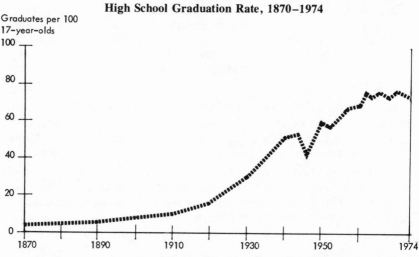

Chart by World Education, 1978 (*The Condition of Education*, 1976, p. 7).

The median level of school completion—how much schooling is completed by half the adult population—is also rising. Figure 2 shows the median level of school completion for those aged 25 and over, both males and females, all races.

When we use the criterion of high school completion to help delineate the population that has not achieved functional literacy, we arrive at essentially the same figure as that arrived at by those who used competency levels: somewhere between 54 and 64 million. The total population of the United States in 1978 is estimated to be about 218 million. Of these, about 70 percent, 152.5 million, are "adult"; that is, 16 years or older. About 70 million of these adults have completed high school. Some 26 million are still in the educational system, in high schools, colleges and universities, or training schools of one kind or another. Those who most concern us are persons 16 and over who are not enrolled in school and have less than a high school education. The U.S. Bureau of Labor Statistics estimates their number at about 57,654,000, or 38 percent of the total population 16 and over (*Special Labor Force Report*, 1976). The figures were confirmed in a 1974 state-by-state analysis by the National Advisory Council on Adult Education (1974, pp. 101–151).[4]

---

[4]The U.S. Office of Education uses the figure 54 million. The most recent NACAE figures suggest that the numbers may be as high as 65 million.

FIGURE 2

Median Level of School Completion (Aged 25 and Over, All Races), 1950–1975

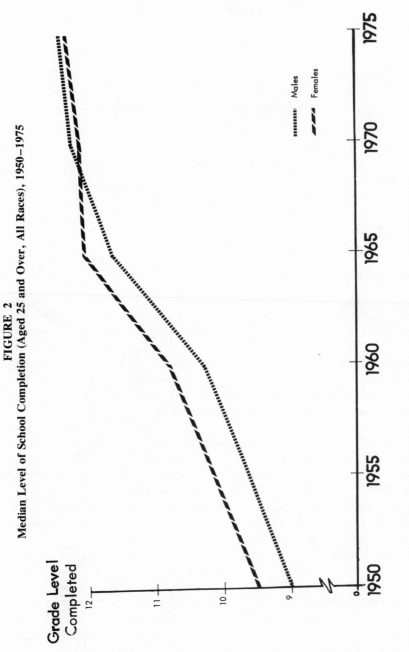

Figure by World Education, 1978 (Based on data from *Current Population Reports*, p-20, #295, 1976).

FIGURE 3
High School Completion, 1978

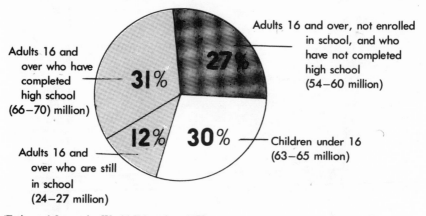

Adults 16 and over, not enrolled in school, and who have not completed high school (54–60 million)

Adults 16 and over who have completed high school (66–70) million)

Adults 16 and over who are still in school (24–27 million)

Children under 16 (63–65 million)

(Estimated figures by World Education, 1978)

We concentrate on those with less than a high school education primarily because more comparative figures are available. We do so, however, realizing that our focus on this group is arbitrary. It is clear that completion of high school is not a reliable indicator of functional literacy. It is equally clear that many persons who have not completed high school, or even grade school, are in fact functioning in ways that bring them personal satisfaction and contribute to their families' and society's well-being.

Three sets of data support this argument. Employment figures of March 1975 show, in general, that the higher rates of unemployment are among those with less than a high school education; the very highest rate of joblessness, however, is not among those with fewer than five years of school, as might be expected, but rather among high school drop-outs. Second, among men between the ages of 25 and 54 with fewer than five years of school, 89 percent were in the labor force. Finally, one researcher showed that although many recruits in low-level military occupations were unable to read the materials deemed necessary, they nevertheless performed their jobs adequately (Sticht, 1975). All these clues suggest that large numbers of persons who have less than a high school education are in fact functioning in this society. At what level, and with what degree of personal satisfaction, of course, the statistics do not tell us.

Where Are They?

Those persons in our society who lack sufficient reading and writing skills to function effectively are found in large numbers wherever there are poor people and wherever there are congregated racial and ethnic minority groups. They are found in city ghettos and doing hard physical labor on unmechanized farms. There are more of them, both in absolute numbers and in percentages, in the South than in the North, more in the East than in the West.

Figure 4 is a map of the United States showing by state the percentage of adults over 16 who have less than a high school education. In nine states, all in the South, over 50 percent of the adults have not completed high school.

Nationwide, statistics are high even for those who have not completed grade school. The National Center for Educational Statistics (NCES) estimated that, in 1976, "the percentage of the adult population over 17 with an eighth grade education or less was 18.1 percent."[5]

In 1970 an estimated 16 million adults—11.3 percent of the adult population—had less than a fifth-grade education.
Two million adult Americans never attended any school at all[6]
(*The Condition of Education*, 1976)

If we look at adults 25 and over who have not completed grade school, regional differences are striking (Figure 5).

If we can trust the figures, it appears that in the South well over 20 percent of the adults have not completed the eighth grade.

Table 2 shows the numbers of persons involved. In the South, 42 percent of the adults 25 and over who might be considered educationally disadvantaged (that is, who did not complete high school) have had fewer than eight years of schooling. Twenty-one of the fifty states have a million or more adults who have not completed high school and who are not currently enrolled in

---

[5]In 1975, the U.S. Bureau of Labor Statistics, presumably working from more-or-less the same census data, arrived at 9 percent of the population over 16, or a total of 14,153,000.

[6]Although this number probably includes immigrants, a large number of elderly people, and those with severe physical and mental handicaps, it is interesting to note that NCES reports that almost two million children between the ages of seven and seventeen were not enrolled in school in 1970 (*The Condition of Education*, 1976, p. 63).

FIGURE 4

Less Than High School Completion: Regional Differences

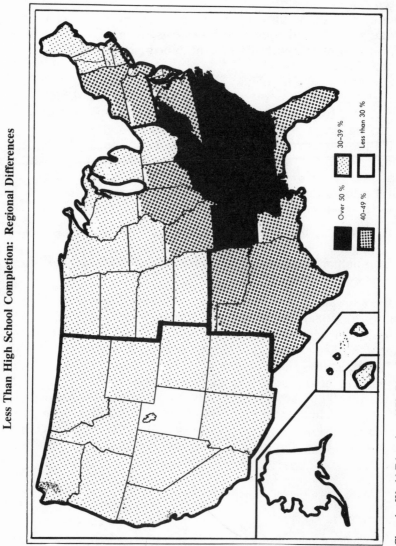

30–39 %

Less than 30 %

Over 50 %

40–49 %

Chart by World Education, 1978 (Data from NACAE, 1974, pp. 101–151).

FIGURE 5
Less Than Grade School Completion: Regional Differences

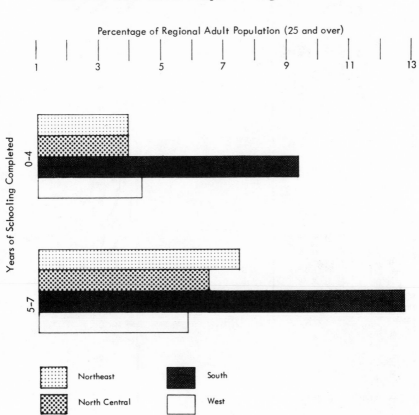

Chart by World Education, 1978 (Based on *Current Population Reports*, p-20, #295, 1976).

school. They are, by and large, those states with the largest total populations (Figure 6).

More undereducated adults live in urban than in rural areas—62 percent to 38 percent, respectively. Some 27 million are in cities, 17 million in "nonmetropolitan areas." Over 15 percent of adults in rural areas have not even completed grade school. In general, those who live in the suburbs stay in school longer than those who live either in the inner city or in rural areas. As Table 3 shows, in rural areas only about 46 percent complete high school, whereas in suburban areas the percentage is 70; in central cities, 61. Of the total suburban population, only about

TABLE 2
Grade Completion Level by Region, 1975
(aged 25 and over, both sexes, all races)

	Less Than Grade School		Less Than High School
North Central	2,359,000	or 21 percent of	11,306,000
Northeast	2,792,000	or 27 percent of	10,386,000
West	1,649,000	or 28 percent of	5,974,000
South	6,749,000	or 42 percent of	16,147,000
TOTALS	13,549,000		43,813,000

SOURCE: *Current Population Reports*, P-20, #295, 1976.

TABLE 3
Urban/Rural Distribution: Less Than High School Completion, 1975
(Aged 25 and over, both sexes, all races), in percentages

	Years of schooling completed			
	0–4	5–7	8	9–11
Urban	5	7.8	9.6	16.4
Suburban	2.3	4.9	8.2	14.3
Rural	5.6	9.8	13.3	16.3

SOURCE: Based on data from *Current Population Reports*, P-20, #295, 1976.

FIGURE 6

States With More Than 1,000,000 Adults With Less Than High School Completion

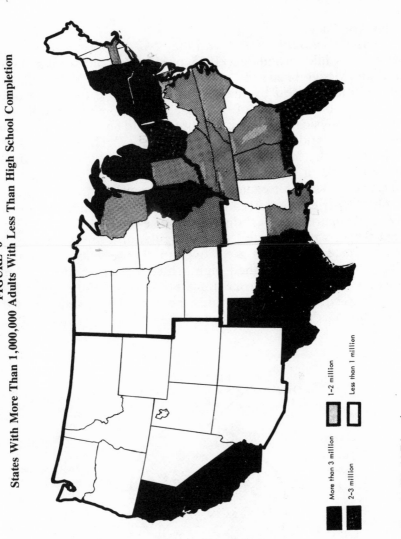

More than 3 million

2-3 million

1-2 million

Less than 1 million

Chart by World Education

7 percent have not completed grade school; in rural areas failure to finish grade school is more than double that percentage.

Table 4 ranks the states and the District of Columbia, as of 1974, by the percentage of adults over 16 with less than high school completion.

Who Are They?

In their valuable small volume, *The Information Poor in America*, Childers and Post (1975, p. 11) report on the information and knowledge needs of "disadvantaged adults." They discuss the problems faced by the deaf and blind and list those other groups that "by virtue of their social, economic, cultural, educational, physical, or ethnic condition could be expected to suffer more deprivation than the rest of society." Their list includes "the poor, the imprisoned, the elderly, the undereducated, the unemployed or those employed at a low level (unskilled and migrant workers, for example), and the racially . . . oppressed."

Our experience and reading confirm their findings. Both the available figures and descriptive and case-study materials suggest that there is no discrete "target population" on whom we can focus. Instead, there is great overlap. Those who are poor are likely not to have finished high school. Blacks and ethnic minorities make up a disproportionate number of the poor and the unemployed. Figure 7 illustrates the overlapping spheres of the disadvantaged.

FIGURE 7
The Overlapping Spheres of the Disadvantaged

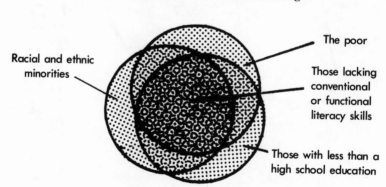

Chart by World Education, 1978.

We have come to understand that the undereducated, with whom we are especially concerned, are also primarily the poor and racial and ethnic minorities. In the sections that follow we shall look at how the figures about educational achievement (primarily grade-completion statistics) relate to these two groups and to other socially disadvantaged groups.

THE POOR

"Poverty," like "illiteracy," is not clearly defined. It, too, is relative and changes at different times and among different cultures. That poor people are unlikely to have high levels of formal schooling and that illiterate persons in our society are likely to be poor are relationships so well accepted as hardly to need verification. But perhaps other questions should be borne in mind. Which is the relevant fact: That good jobs and high pay are rewards for staying in school? Or that well-to-do families tend to keep their children in school longer? To what extent does school completion depend on economic factors?

Income

Of the 54.3 million persons 16 and over in 1970 who were not enrolled in school and who had less than a high school education, 75 percent earned less than $5,000 a year. Only 1 percent had incomes of $15,000 or more, compared to about 33 percent of all families in the United States (NACAE, 1974, p. 33). When average income is correlated with levels of schooling, we find significant differences between those with less formal education and those with more. Those who have completed high school have incomes about double those who have not completed grade school, and half again higher than those with eighth grade education. This situation prevails among all sectors of the population: men and women, white and black, and all age groups (ibid., p. 32). Those whose schooling stopped before the eighth grade have lifetime earnings about one-third of those with graduate study: in 1970, $250,000 contrasted to $800,000, a gap apparently widening (ibid.). Finally, Figure 8 shows the clear relationship between weekly earnings and years of schooling for white male workers aged 35 to 44 in May 1973.

Figure 9 demonstrates that the same relationship applies to percentages of families considered to be living below the government-defined poverty level ($4,275 for a nonfarm family of four, in 1972).

TABLE 4

States Ranked According to Percentage of Adult Population With Less Than High School Completion, 1974

Rank STATE	Percent of Adult Population With Less Than High School Completion	Total Adult Population	Rank by Population	Adult Population with Less Than High School Completion
1. Kentucky	53.3	2,229,676	23	1,188,000
2. South Carolina	52.4	1,745,829	26	916,775
3. North Carolina	52.2	3,523,870	12	1,841,581
4. Arkansas	52.1	1,342,032	32	700,712
5. Georgia	51.0	3,122,093	15	1,595,415
6. Mississippi	50.7	1,466,697	29	744,623
7. Alabama	50.7	2,349,346	21	1,191,792
8. Tennessee	50.5	2,745,755	17	1,387,575
9. West Virginia	50.3	1,233,143	34	621,314
10. Louisiana	49.1	2,403,840	20	1,180,582
11. Rhode Island	45.3	679,180	39	308,215
12. Texas	45.1	7,635,716	4	3,445,926
13. Virginia	44.6	3,232,792	14	1,442,498
14. Missouri	43.8	3,295,492	13	1,446,397
15. Pennsylvania	42.4	8,387,998	3	3,561,337
16. Florida	42.0	4,912,428	9	2,066,790
17. Oklahoma	41.3	1,818,792	27	752,702
18. New York	41.1	12,992,198	2	5,344,393
19. New Jersey	41.1	5,040,321	8	2,073,023
20. Maryland	40.8	2,686,019	18	1,096,992
21. Illinois	40.7	7,727,579	5	3,147,456
22. Indiana	40.3	3,556,767	11	1,433,705
23. North Dakota	39.9	418,076	46	167,179
24. Michigan	39.9	5,979,788	7	2,386,301
25. Ohio	39.7	7,325,568	6	2,909,938

26.	Maine	38.9	686,206	38	267,276
27.	Delaware	38.8	371,657	47	144,052
28.	District of Columbia	38.7	555,869	41	215,018
29.	South Dakota	38.1	453,328	45	173,397
30.	Connecticut	37.7	2,120,413	24	800,073
31.	New Mexico	37.6	653,939	37	246,992
32.	Wisconsin	37.5	3,008,537	16	1,128,138
33.	New Hampshire	36.7	509,150	42	187,051
34.	Iowa	36.3	1,960,685	25	713,982
35.	Arizona	36.2	1,196,750	33	433,126
36.	Vermont	35.8	304,409	49	109,528
37.	Massachusetts	35.2	4,015,691	10	1,415,564
38.	Minnesota	34.5	2,576,109	19	890,660
39.	Montana	34.2	471,050	44	161,254
40.	Idaho	34.2	480,322	43	164,279
41.	Kansas	33.8	1,586,294	28	536,994
42.	Nebraska	33.8	1,033,538	35	349,615
43.	Oregon	33.7	1,479,103	31	499,503
44.	California	32.1	14,051,516	1	4,513,145
45.	Wyoming	31.4	226,440	50	71,669
46.	Hawaii	30.9	523,055	40	161,899
47.	Nevada	30.8	335,551	48	103,359
48.	Washington	30.8	2,383,207	22	733,709
49.	Colorado	30.3	1,518,799	30	461,261
50.	Alaska	28.5	191,337	51	54,663
51.	Utah	26.2	682,543	36	179,743

TOTAL 55,880,571

SOURCE: Based on data from NACAE, 1974, pp. 101–151.

FIGURE 8
Weekly Earnings Related to Years of Schooling, May 1973
(White Males 35–44)

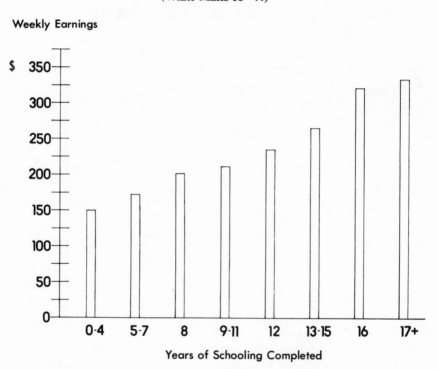

Weekly Earnings

Years of Schooling Completed

Chart by World Education, 1978 (Based on data from NACAE, 1974, p. 33).

FIGURE 9
Poverty Related to Years of Schooling

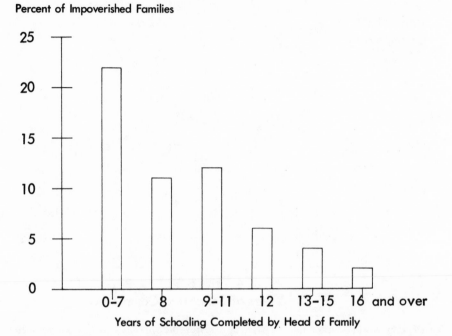

Percent of Impoverished Families

Years of Schooling Completed by Head of Family

Chart by World Education, 1978 (Based on data from NACAE, 1974, p. 32).

NOTE: There is an officially defined poverty threshold which is adjusted each year for changes in the consumer price index. In 1972 it stood at $4,275 for a nonfarm family of four (NACAE, 1974, p. 32).

Employment

While it is true that the more education one has, the more likely one is to be an active member of the labor force, and while employment rates of adults who have graduated from high school are about double those who have not, the figures do not correlate directly to years of schooling completed, as Figure 10 shows. True, unemployment rates are lowest for college graduates, but they are not highest, as one might have expected, for those with almost no formal schooling, but for high school drop-outs. In March 1975, when the overall unemployment rate was 9.2 percent of the labor force, the unemployment rates of high school drop-outs were considerably higher than for those who had completed a lower grade. The latter, in turn, were also somewhat above the national level in unemployment.

FIGURE 10
Unemployment Related to Years of Schooling, 1975

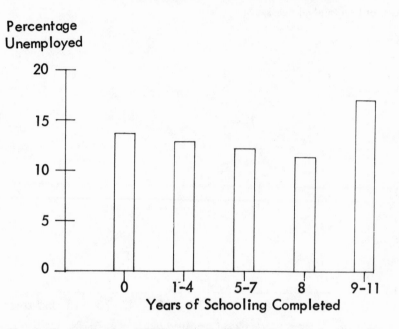

Chart by World Education, 1978 (Based on data from the *Special Labor Force Report No. 186*, 1976).

There are a number of possible reasons why the unemployment rates tend to be higher for high school drop-outs than for those with less education. First, many of those with less than an eighth grade education are not in the labor force at all. Those who are tend to be older, more experienced workers whose lack of formal education may be offset by their on-the-job experience. Figure 10 shows the unemployment rates of all workers at a particular time; Table 5 looks at the hard-core unemployed—those who, in March 1975, had been unemployed for 15 weeks or more. Thus, those without jobs who have completed eighth grade or less tend to remain unemployed for longer periods than do high school drop-outs or the population at large.

Public Assistance

One other indicator often used to underline the problems faced by those in our society with less than a high school education is their appearance on the public welfare rolls. Although people

TABLE 5
Hard-Core Unemployment, March 1975

Years of Schooling Completed	Unemployment Rate
0–4	35.6
5–8	35.2
9–11	28.3

SOURCE: Based on data from *Special Labor Force Report No. 186,* 1976.

go on welfare for a wide variety of reasons, across the board, for men and women, for blacks and whites, and for all age groups, a prime common denominator is the level of schooling attained. The proportion of persons with fewer than six grades of school on public assistance is more than double that among those with six to eight years and almost four times that among those with nine to eleven years of school (NACAE, 1974, p. 20).

RACIAL AND ETHNIC MINORITIES

The available statistics reveal additionally even more disturbing interrelationships among poverty, education, and racial/ethnic origin. Across all levels of education minority group members rank lower than majority group members.

In all parts of the country, but particularly in rural areas, the number of blacks and other minorities among the educationally disadvantaged is disproportionately high. Among rural blacks, for instance, 45 percent have not completed grade school; for the population as a whole the figure is about 15 percent. (The comparison figures for rural whites are not available.) Figure 11 breaks the figures down into urban/suburban/rural populations. (Although the figures are for those over 25 rather than 16, the proportions are indicative.)

Blacks, of course, are by no means the only educationally disadvantaged racial or ethnic group. Hispanic groups, especially Hispanic women, have a noticeably lower level of educational attainment than either whites or blacks. All those for whom English is not the mother tongue—about 30 million Americans, or 13 percent—face special educational difficulties. This includes the large but unknown number of illegal aliens, mostly Spanish-speaking.[7] The 827,000 Native Americans also face special prob-

---

[7]The 130,000 refugees from Vietnam, Laos, and Cambodia have been targeted for special services through the Emergency Adult Education Program for Indo-Chinese Refugees.

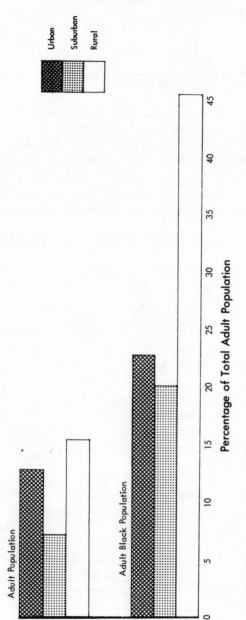

FIGURE 11

Less Than Grade School Completion: Blacks in Relation to Total Population, 1970

Chart by World Education, 1978 (Based on data from *Current Population Reports*, P-20, #295, 1976).

lems. Only 40 percent of adult urban Native Americans, and fewer than 25 percent of those who live in rural areas, have graduated from high school. Their representation in the work force is so low that they generally do not even appear on the charts. Even in such a central working age group as 35–44, the labor market participation rates for Native American males with fewer than 12 years of schooling is only 63 percent, compared with 86 percent for blacks and 93 percent for whites of the same age and similar schooling.[8] Among those for whom figures are available, Mexican Americans, many of whom are employed as migrant workers, leave school at the earliest ages. Table 6 sums up the limited data available.

Incomes of blacks rise as educational levels rise, but remain below that of whites of similar educational achievements. Figure 8 showed weekly earnings of white males aged 35 to 44 in May 1973 and related those earnings to years of schooling completed. Figure 12 displays the weekly earning figures for black males in the same age group.

Unemployment rates for high school drop-outs, displayed in Figure 14, are consistently higher for blacks than for whites.

The median family income for all Americans in 1970 was about $9,600, an increase of 70 percent in ten years. The median income for blacks during the decade rose at an even faster rate: from just over $3,000 in 1960 to about $6,000 in 1970. The median income of black families, however, still fell far short of the median of about $10,000 for white families.

The median level of school completion is also rising, and not only for whites. Figure 14 looks at adults over 25 and compares

TABLE 6
Median Years of Schooling by Race/Ethnicity, 1970

	White	Black	Other Spanish-Speaking	Mexican
Urban	12.4	11.7	9.3	8.7
Suburban	12.5	11.6	11.5	9.6
Rural	12.2	8.4	7.5	6.7
Average total	12.4	11.0	9.6	8.5

SOURCE: Based on data from *Current Population Reports,* P-20, #295, 1976.

---

[8]Note that we do not equate successful functioning or leading creative and productive lives in their own communities or in the larger society with participation in the labor force by Native Americans or by any other group. We are simply using the available statistical data for what they can tell us.

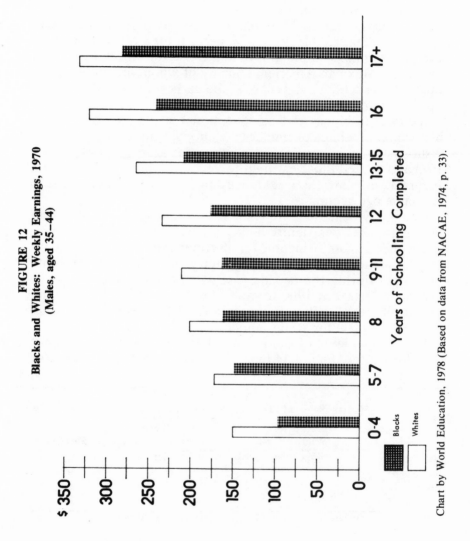

FIGURE 12
Blacks and Whites: Weekly Earnings, 1970
(Males, aged 35–44)

Years of Schooling Completed

Chart by World Education, 1978 (Based on data from NACAE, 1974, p. 33).

FIGURE 13

Unemployment Rates for High School Dropouts, 1968–1975

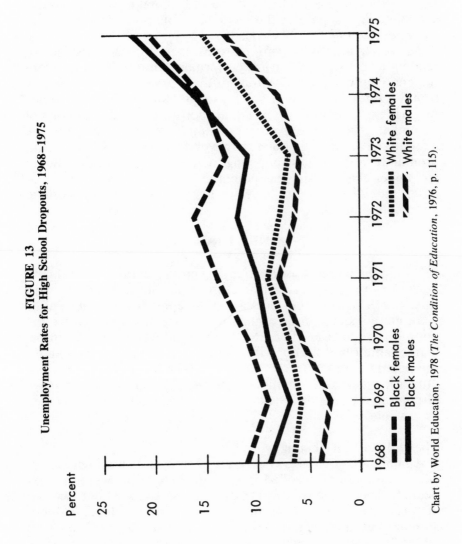

Chart by World Education, 1978 (*The Condition of Education*, 1976, p. 115).

the median level of school completion for whites with that of
blacks and Hispanics.

For blacks, the rise in median level of school completion is
dramatic—from 5 years and 8 months in 1940 to 11 years in 1975.
Indeed, the gap has gradually narrowed so that only half a year's
schooling now separates the medians of blacks and whites (12.1
as opposed to 12.5) (NACAE, 1974, p. 7).

As we have noted, hiring patterns seem to be related not to
reading levels needed for job performance but, rather, to years
of schooling completed. Although there are signs of a changing
trend, whites still stay in school longer than blacks and other
minorities. This and other social factors inevitably favor the
dominant groups in our society. Simply put, poor parents are
likely to have less schooling than well-to-do-parents. Their children, in turn, have less schooling than the children of the middle
and upper classes, and less potential for upward social and economic mobility. And they are more likely to be members of ethnic
and racial minorities.

OTHER GROUPS

Within the three major overlapping groups of the educationally
deprived—the poor, racial and ethnic minorities, and those with
less than a high school education—are subgroups who suffer
from more specific disadvantages. Primary among these are the
young, the old, the imprisoned, and women. Statistical information about these groups is even more elusive than data about
the population as a whole. We strongly believe, however, that
efforts must be made to understand their special situations as we
attempt to address the needs of the educationally disadvantaged
as a whole.

The Old And The Young

Among adults 16 years and over with less than a high school
education and not enrolled in school, there is, as would be expected, a heavy concentration of older persons. About two out
of three are 45 and over; one in four is 65 or older. Table 7
summarizes the grade-level achievement by age group of all
adults 16 years and over with less than a high school education
and not enrolled in school. Of those with less than a high school
education, more than three-quarters of those 65 and over have not
completed grade school.

Unemployment rates and public assistance rates are also dis-

FIGURE 14

Minority Groups and Whites: Median Level of School Completion
(Aged 25 and Over, 1950–1975)

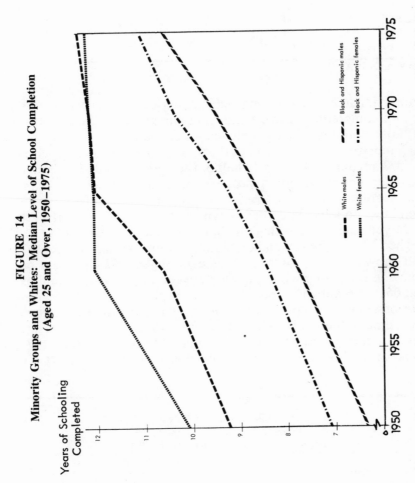

Chart by World Education, 1978 (Based on data from *Current Population Reports*, T-20, #295, 1976).

TABLE 7
Grade-level Achievement by Age
(Groups with less than high school education)

Age	Total	Total years of schooling completed		
		0–5	6–8	9–11
TOTAL	100%	3%	53%	44%
16–24	100	4	24	72
25–34	100	3	31	66
35–44	100	2	42	56
45–64	100	2	56	42
65+	100	5	73	22

SOURCE: NACAE, 1974, p. 10.

proportionately high among older Americans at every level of school completion. Table 8 indicates the public assistance rates of those with less than a high school education.

Comprising only a quarter of the total labor force, young people in 1972 accounted for nearly half of the unemployed. The impact has been devastatingly disproportionate in black and other minority communities, where in some areas over half the young men have no jobs. The unemployment rate for older youths (20- to 24-year-olds) is also higher than it was a few years ago.

The U.S. Bureau of Labor Statistics reported figures for 1977 that showed unemployment rates even higher; 42.1 percent nationwide for young white people between the ages of 16 and 19, and 66.3 percent for minorities. New York City had the highest rate of youth unemployment among 11 major American cities, according to the study, which counted everyone of working age, not only those who were actively looking for jobs. In June 1977, 74 percent of New York City whites between the ages of 16 and

TABLE 8
Public Assistance Rates
Years of Schooling Completed
(Percentage on public assistance, 1970)

Age	0–5	6–8	9–11
TOTAL	15%	7%	4%
16–24	6	6	4
25–34	9	6	6
35–44	12	5	4
45–64	12	3	4
65+	21	11	8

SOURCE: NACAE, 1974, p. 20.

19 and 86 percent of blacks in the same age group did not have a full-time job (*New York Times*, Aug. 2, 1977b, p. 30).

Between 1965 and 1973, over 3.1 million young people between 16 and 21 years old dropped out of high school. In the period 1974 to 1975, 25.3 percent of all drop-outs between the ages of 16 and 24 were unemployed; 61.4 percent of those nonwhites who dropped out of school were unemployed.

Even completing high school does not adequately prepare young people for the job market or assure them of work for which they are prepared. One educator recommended strongly that blacks and other minority youngsters go to college. If they do not, he said, "they will never—or may never—get a job." He concluded:

> Trying to encourage minority youngsters to get an education, learn good work habits and seek employment that holds little for the future, while bombarding them every day with television and film images of success, mostly illegal, some legal, without telling them "how to" become legally successful, is [probably] impossible to do.
> . . . Soon the suffering youngsters of today will marry and have children who in a few years will inherit the problems of their parents, and the vicious circle will go on: poor education, lack of training, jobless youngsters, continuing welfare drain, chaos (Hodgkinson, 1977).

The Imprisoned

Persons who have been imprisoned have lower levels of educational achievement than the population at large. About 75 percent have not completed high school, as opposed to 38 percent of the total adult population. Some 35 to 42 percent have an eighth grade education or less. These figures are based on information from the 1970 census on educational levels for prisoners over 25. Because some 26 percent of all persons in prisons and jails are between the ages of 20 and 24, and because there is another large group of youthful offenders between 16 and 20 for whom figures were not available, these percentages may be somewhat skewed.

Table 9 shows the Law Enforcement Assistance Administration (LEAA) figures for jail inmates as of 1972. These figures do not jibe with the census figures for 1970, which showed a total of about 98,000 persons over 25 with less than a high school education in federal prisons plus an additional 51,000 in state, city, and county jails, for a total of 149,000 (of a total prison population of

TABLE 9
Prison Population: Years of Schooling Completed, 1972

Years of Schooling	Black	White	Total
0–8	19,000	25,000	44,000
9–11	51,000	37,000	88,000
Total less than high school	70,000	62,000	132,000

SOURCE: Law Enforcement Assistance Administration, 1972.

205,000). We are left with these inconsistent figures pending further research.

Women
    Until recently, as Figures 3 and 15 showed, the median level of school completion was higher for women than men. This remains true for black and Hispanic women, but during the mid-1960s the pattern changed for whites. Between 1960 and 1970 (possibly to avoid or postpone being drafted) white young men began staying in school longer. The median level of school completion for white men jumped one-and-a-half grade levels in this decade, from 10.8 to 12.2. In 1970, the median school completion for white men and women was the same, 12.2. By 1978, men were staying in school longer. Of the population over 25 who have not completed high school, 20 million are men; 22 million are women. Of those who have an eighth grade education or less, more are men than women (6.7 million compared to 5.8 million). But of those who dropped out of high school, many more are women (10.3 million women to 7.9 million men).[9]
    Despite their relatively higher level of schooling, women, as we know, have not participated in the labor force nor commanded salaries commensurate with their education. Women outnumbered men in participation in adult basic education (ABE) courses in 1970 by as much as 57 percent to 43 percent. As the National Advisory Council on Adult Education points out, "Certainly the economic benefits could not be that much of a lure." The 1970 census showed that white males with less than a grade school education earned a mean income of about $4,600; this rose to over $6,100 among those who completed eighth grade, an increase of about $1,500 a year. For women, however, the comparable figures are $2,000 and $2,400, an increase of $400 (NACAE, 1974, p. 73).

---

[9]These figures can be explained only partly by the relative population numbers, that is, by the fact that, because women live longer than men, women outnumber men in the total population by about 100 to 94.8.

Despite the changes in federal legislation and policy prohibiting discrimination in hiring and wages, the earning gap between men and women has grown. Differences in pay based on sex are still larger than those based on race or national origin—particularly for working class women. As the environment changes and more support becomes available, however, they and their advocates will be able to press a large agenda of essential reforms at every level of American society. We know that early school tracking practices have negative effects on poor children (Persell, 1977). These are especially serious for lower-class girls who for years have been placed in courses in homemaking skills. For working women with little formal education engaged in service jobs, the difference between their salaries and those of men in the same work was 63 percent. For sales workers it was 57 percent and for assembly-line workers 41 percent. For women with five or more years of college the average gap between their salaries and men's (of equal education) was 35 percent. For women with four years of high school it was 42 percent and increased as the level of education attainment was lowered (Seifer, 1973).

Because few working women are members of unions (only one in seven) and because only one out of five union members is a woman, unions do not offer them much protection. Both external factors and internal psychological pressures keep women from challenging the status quo, although change may result from the current efforts of caucuses of women union members.

Working class women suffer disproportionately from economic marginality, unsatisfying jobs, poor working conditions, inadequate social and municipal services, deteriorating neighborhoods, and alienation from the American mainstream. Limited education and limited experience outside the home have held these women back. The situation is particularly difficult for those women who are the sole support for their families. Heretofore they have lacked any sense that the women's movement spoke for them. Although heightened consciousness from the largely middle-class women's movement has stimulated activity among women for whom new educational, job-training, and skill-development opportunities have long been available, the leadership potential of working class women has been systematically overlooked.

BEYOND THE STATISTICS

The statistical information, unreliable and limited though it is, bears out our basic thesis: People who lack basic or functional literacy skills are surprisingly large in number and also suffer from other major social and economic disadvantages.

Other information, perhaps more helpful, about the characteristics shared by most of the educationally impaired has appeared in sociological and anthropological studies, some in oral histories. These writings bring us closer to a gut understanding of what a low level of literacy may mean in people's lives.

The Information Poor in America gives us a portrait of the disadvantaged American "in his natural information habitat. . . . The prototypal disadvantaged American, . . . more than his average counterpart":

> Does not know which formal channels to tap in order to solve his problems, or what specific programs exist to respond to his needs;
> Watches many hours of television daily, seldom reads newspapers and magazines and never reads books;
> Does not see his problems as information needs;
> Is not a very active information seeker, even when he does undertake a search;
> May lean heavily on formal channels of information if it becomes apparent that the informal channels are inadequate and if his needs are strongly felt;
> Is locked into an informal information network that is deficient in the information that is ordinarily available to the rest of society. (Childers, 1975, pp. 42–43).

Jack Mezirow of Teachers College, Columbia University, has also added to our understanding of the multiple disadvantages of those who lack conventional or functional literacy skills. Mezirow speaks of "the future syndrome endemic to ghetto, barrio, and reservation—a continually reinforced conviction of failure and incompetence, bred by a grim history of frustrating school experiences and subsequent inability to support oneself and one's family, which becomes a self-fulfilling prophecy." His description of a 45-year-old black man evokes for us an image of what such a life is really like:

> eking out a living at an unstable succession of menial and arduous jobs, poor, haunted by failure, numbed with self-doubt, without study skills, and unable to read. Furthermore, going back to school seems an endless uphill struggle. Just learning the three R's means years of weary plugging, night after night, month after month. And then what? What will an eighth-grade education get you? Into the ninth grade is about all (Mezirow, et al., 1975, pp. 37–38).

One attempt to describe "the disadvantaged adult" that many educators found helpful in explaining their own experiences was the work of the Appalachian Adult Education Center (AAEC). After seven years of intensive work with disadvantaged adults, whom they define as "those over 16 years of age, who are (1) out of school, with less than a high school diploma, and/or (2) with a family income below a poverty index," George Eyster and his colleagues at the AAEC identified four groups, each with special needs and requiring different approaches and different services. The four groups are based on individual characteristics; indeed, members of different groups are often found in the same family. Individuals also fluctuate between groups at different times in their lives, or as their circumstances change.

Persons in the first two groups are the easiest to reach. Group 1 consists of "secure" and "self-directed" persons who respond well to group activities as well as to individualized instruction and are open to recruitment through the media. Group 2 consists of persons less economically and personally secure—those with large families and seasonal jobs, who must often work overtime. They have suffered some of the consequences of undereducation and underemployment and yet are eager learners capable of quickly achieving specific goals they set for themselves to improve their daily lives. The major difficulty in extending services to persons in this group is time; it is impractical to set rigid hours for class instruction for them because they do not know when they will have to work or tend to family responsibilities.

The third and fourth groups require more specialized instruction. Persons in Group 3 have been only sporadically employed in low-paying, short-term jobs. If they are to be reached, they need individualized recruitment contacts and one-to-one instruction. Group 4 consists of those most in need of, yet least accessible to service. The AAEC calls them "the stationary poor." They, too, require one-to-one instruction. Only by intensive attention will they be reached by any educational program.

Finally, we must add a note of caution. Those of us who prepare studies about disadvantaged people run the risk of perpetuating stereotypes. We tend to simplify complex lives into cases to be analyzed, or problems that need solutions, or statistics to be studied. This tendency, and our inability to interpret with understanding the first-hand information that people give us about their aspirations and their lives, are serious blind spots. It may well be that we can obtain a truer picture, or at least a fuller understanding, from reading Oscar Lewis's *La Vida* (1968), Lillian Breslow Rubin's *Worlds of Pain* (1976), Elliot Liebow's *Tally's Corner* (1967), or Susan Sheehan's *A Welfare Mother* (1976) than from pondering accumulated masses of statistics.

Summary

One fact emerges clearly from all the statistical information available, whether the measure is competency or school completion. Despite the universal free education available in this country since early in the century, despite the fact that more and more young people of all races and ethnic groups are completing high school, and despite the recent evidence that those who do complete high school are achieving "acceptable" levels of literacy, a disproportionately large section of our adult population—well over a third—still suffers some educational disadvantage (Fisher, 1978). Among these millions of adults in our society are the functionally illiterate. Their exact number is not known.

We conclude that the aggregate message of all the statistics is more important than their specific accuracy. A much larger proportion of the U.S. population than had until recently been known or assumed suffers serious disadvantage because of limited educational attainment. In this country persons with limited education are often the same persons who suffer from one or more of the other major social disadvantages—poverty, unemployment, racial or ethnic discrimination, social isolation. Inadequate education will probably be only one manifestation of their deprivation. The greater the number of those disadvantages, the more serious the suffering for members of our society in which one's worth is judged by one's job, possessions, and credentials.

In the next chapter we will examine the currently available programs that are trying to meet the educational needs of the millions in our society whose opportunities are limited by the lack of conventional or functional literacy skills.

CHAPTER
III

✍

What Is Being Done About Adult Illiteracy?

They meet in public schools and churches, union halls and learning centers, offices and factories, museums and storefronts, prisons and libraries, hospitals and homes. They are an astonishing mixture of racial and ethnic backgrounds, educational levels, experiences, and ages. These adults—or their friends and family who urge them on—believe that educational programs may make some difference in their lives. They may learn to read with the help of a tutor. They may read better, compute more easily, communicate more clearly. Some seek the credentials they are always being asked to produce and cannot.

Many lack the physical and emotional stamina required by long hours and slow progress. They drop out—as they have before. The amazing fact, perhaps, is that many others do stick with the programs long enough to fulfill some of their hopes.

One thing is apparent: publicly proclaimed program goals and actual achievements are far apart. The "inability to get or retain employment" will not be eliminated for adult basic education (ABE) participants. Illiteracy will not be "defeated in ten years" by the Right to Read program. Such goals are rhetoric designed to secure legislation and funding from a Congress that knows little about its educationally and economically marginal constituents.

In this chapter we sketch in broad strokes a representative group of programs that are available to adults in the United States who desire, for whatever reasons, to decrease the disadvantages they suffer because of low levels of educational attainment or because English is not their native tongue.

Educators often speak of "target populations," meaning all those who might legitimately be considered candidates for certain programs. During the last decade the approximately 60 million American adults who had not completed high school were designated the target population for ABE and a host of smaller programs designed to promote literacy or to provide credentials. The term *demand population* refers to those who actually enroll in these programs; a group estimated at between 2 and 4 million adults in the United States. The 50 million–plus gap between the target and demand populations is perceived as a major challenge to adult educators. How can it be narrowed? How can a larger proportion of the approximately 60 million "targets" be motivated to enroll and remain in programs? Of course, these questions assume that everyone should be literate and that everyone without a high school diploma should seek one.

Not all adults in the target group will pursue these goals. Many will never enroll in programs of any sort for diverse reasons: cultural or linguistic barriers, fear of failing, distrust of the institutions of the mainstream culture, reliance on electronic media as a substitute for the written word, and the ability of some to find satisfaction despite low levels of academic attainment. Some adults seek functional skills that promise more immediate payoffs—job training, child-care and health information, citizen and consumer information. Others seek assistance with personal and community concerns from religious and cultural institutions. Our definitions of conventional and functional literacy emphasize *self-determined* educational objectives and, therefore, the legitimacy of diverse routes.

How can the various programs be evaluated? Certainly not in the terms of political rhetoric or measured against the broad social reform they promise. The more important questions are whether program objectives are realistic, whether they are clearly communicated, and whether those who participate make visible and satisfying progress. Another aspect to be considered in evaluating these programs is whether, in the aggregate, they conform to what the target population needs and desires. A further consideration is how well programs incorporate what is known about adult learning. The adults who participate in the programs we discuss do not start from scratch. They bring with them their lifelong experience of *informal learning* from many sources. They bring, also, the *socially directed learning* gained within their families and communities, as well as what the larger society has provided through the diverse and sometimes conflicting campaigns of those who promote products or ideas. Many adults have also engaged in *self-directed learning* by deliberately seeking information or skills from more experienced friends and colleagues. The majority bring a residue of experiences, feelings, and learnings from earlier involvements with organized education, either in *formal* schools or in *nonformal* programs outside the school system.[1]

With all these considerations in mind we have organized this chapter on programs and services into three categories. First, programs that have as their fundamental goal the development or increase of conventional literacy skills (e.g., tutoring services that focus primarily on the teaching of reading, ABE, Right to Read Program, and others that focus chiefly on reading, writing, communication, and computation skills); second, programs that have a broader goal and focus on functional competencies or on the functional concerns of ethnic or cultural subgroups; third, programs that rely on broadcast media as a delivery system.

Programs in the first category sometimes incorporate functional-skill training, but as a methodology rather than as a central focus. Many programs in the second category, which are based on the development of functional competencies, also provide conventional-literacy training if the necessity for it is revealed when assessing the needs of participants. Literacy training, however, is secondary in terms of the overall objectives of functional programs. In the third category, broadcast media, some programs are academic while others are related to increasing functional skills. Electronic media have also been used to encourage adults to seek help through educational programs.

In summary, we shall look at a variety of representative educational programs not in terms of broad social goals, but, rather, as instruments to enable participants to achieve more limited objectives. What are the programs actually doing to help adults to read and write, to compute and communicate? What functional skills do they offer? In the broad perspective of adult learning

---

[1]We know, too, according to some learning theories, that adults have developed from this long experience information categories or "sets" that make them inclined to reject information that conflicts with their earlier learning. The level of their adult learning effort and degree of achievement will be related to their motivation, the vigor and persistence of their commitment, and their expectation of success as well as to the congruence of the program with their own needs (Broschart, 1976, p. 17).

theory, do they cover the range of needs of the population group they are designed to serve? Are their approaches sufficiently diverse to make them both accessible to and effective for their target constituency?

TUTORING AND BASIC EDUCATION: CATEGORY 1

Our first category, programs that focus on conventional literacy skills, comprises a wide variety of efforts. We begin with the voluntary literacy organizations, then move on to a detailed discussion of ABE, or adult basic education, which is the major operational program in category one. We then sketch the Right to Read programs, programs in prisons and other correctional institutions, and programs in libraries.

Voluntary Literacy Organizations

An aspect of American life that has intrigued foreign observers since Alexis de Tocqueville is the existence of so many wide-ranging voluntary service organizations. Among these are organizations dedicated to teaching reading to youth and adults. Two of the best known are Laubach Literacy, with a long history of literacy campaigns outside the United States and active in this country as the National Affiliation for Literacy Advance (NALA), and Literacy Volunteers of America (LVA). (See *The Educational Programs of Laubach Literacy International*, 1976, and *General Descriptions of Programs and Services*, n.d.) The influence of these two groups goes far beyond the work done by their trained tutors. Their campaigns to recruit volunteers have kept before the public the fact that there are adult Americans who are unable to read. Even persons who know little about such federally funded programs as ABE have heard of Laubach Literacy and LVA. Both have deep roots in the Christian service tradition. They offer a place where it is possible "to start from the very bottom," pointing out that other programs are not elementary enough to meet the needs of the beginning student (Colvin and Root, 1976).

NALA and LVA have their own tutor-training and credentialing systems. LVA's is more closely controlled and monitored by its central staff. NALA relies on local affiliates to certify tutors, although it requires a complicated progression from basic tutor-training through training of trainers. NALA's methods for the teaching of reading have been developed and tested over the years and are carefully spelled out in its publications for teachers and students. LVA offers more diversity of methods. Its published materials are for the use of tutors or for those who run training workshops. In addition, LVA has courses for those interested in setting up and maintaining local LVA literacy programs—with suggestions about recruiting, publicizing the program, operating and reporting, and training tutors. In recent years NALA has emphasized the production of materials, especially easy-to-read materials that Laubach publishes under the New Readers' Press imprint as supplements to Laubach's New Streamlined English Series.

The advertisements for materials from the New Readers' Press include such phrases as "developing coping skills for today's world," but actually the tutor-training is confined to the training of reading specialists. The *Instructor's Aid*, which is available with a weekly newsletter *News For You* (circulation about 60,000), contains exercises and activities that the teacher can use to reinforce reading, writing, and comprehension skills. The materials emphasize mastering print rather than involvement or action. So do the booklets on practical life issues.

NALA staff members informed us that Laubach materials and methods used overseas focus more directly on real-life problems than do those used in this country. Laubach's international programs try to recruit, train, and support tutors "from the student's immediate environment," but in the United States, over 90 percent of its tutors are white females; over 70 percent are between the ages of 40 and 70; 96 percent are high school graduates and 53 percent college graduates (Stauffer, 1973, p. 29). Such a comparison suggests greater disparity in life experience between NALA's American tutors and their students than is the case in its overseas programs, where tutors and teachers are likely to come from the milieu of their students—and may be only a bit ahead of them in reading skills.

Only 8 to 10 percent of the sales of Laubach materials in this country are to NALA affiliates; the rest are to ABE and other public and private organizations teaching reading and working with new readers. In cooperation with the School of Communications at Syracuse University, Robert S. Laubach, son of the founder of Laubach Literacy and NALA, supervises research on teaching methods and materials for new readers, including the actual preparation of materials. The publications are on such topics as consumer economics, health, ecology, civics, vocational and career information, family living, driver education, and other areas of concern to adults. Tutor/teaching-training, however, is confined solely to the teaching of reading. Other organizations that use Laubach materials, including ABE, must provide additional practical training in helping students gain skills in the life-experience areas that are touched on by these materials.

Literacy Volunteers of America (LVA) has published a comprehensive bibliography of reading materials that includes suggestions for basic reading and for English as a second language but does not insist on the use of any specific materials. The organization does require that all tutors have LVA basic training. The LVA course is highly structured; staff members at the national office in Syracuse commented that careful control of training and of the activities of affiliates are the only means they could devise for quality control (*Leaders' Handbook*, 1975).

NALA relies on local organizations which may or may not carry the Laubach name. These local groups are loosely related through annual NALA representational meetings and an executive committee (*The NALA Directory*, 1976). The national office (also in Syracuse) receives reports and, in a sense, keeps the books on what is going on around the country. This office shares information about procedures that have worked, new materials, research findings, and methods for starting work in new areas. Affiliates are individuals who have been trained and are working locally.

LVA's procedures governing affiliates are more carefully worked out. These are organizations based in local communities, staffed by volunteers, and financially self-supporting. Their sole purpose is to carry on its basic reading and conversational English tutoring programs (Colvin, 1976 and Colvin and Root, 1972).

Through single-minded dedication to the teaching of reading to adults with minimal reading skills, both organizations have been able to develop tools of sufficient quality to be used by others who have come more recently to the field. Their long experience in recruiting volunteers has not only produced needed personnel but has in many instances provided warm personal concern, a basic and needed ingredient in reaching adult non-readers. Because the national structure of LVA has more influence over the activities of its affiliated local groups, it seemed to us that they were generally more interested than NALA in tying local LVA activities into ongoing ABE and Right to Read efforts. LVA leaders state clearly that they see their own tutoring and small-group work as a feeder for more advanced work. External testimony from the state education officials in various locations underlined the great importance of this function. LVA has operated many training sessions in basic reading for ABE teachers throughout the country.

Laubach Literacy, on principle, receives no government funding for its central budget, but projects in which its NALA volunteers work are frequently cosponsored by Right to Read and ABE. In fact, while budgets for the central offices of both organizations rely on private donations, both are also able to extend their work and influence by cosponsoring local projects funded by the federal government or by foundations. Laubach's publishing enterprise supplies between 70 and 75 percent of its central budget, $1,254,074 of a total income of $1,759,950 in 1976–77. LVA's annual budget is about $382,000.

Except for projects that these organizations administer, either by themselves or with others, in institutional settings, it is probable that all of these programs are most apt to reach those illiterates who are somewhat atypical in their own environment. Because their families and colleagues are largely literate, they have long been embarrassed by their impediment. It is possible that the generally middle-class tutors and teachers trained by the two organizations would have difficulty working with the "stationary poor"—those hard-core disadvantaged adults who feel hopeless about their ability to change their situation and who do not generally see reading as a means of help.[2]

ABE: The Major Operational Program

ABE (Adult Basic Education) was inaugurated by the *Economic Opportunity Act of 1964*. In 1966, authority for the adult education aspects of the program was transferred to the Office of Education of HEW, under Title III of the *Elementary and Secondary Education Act*. Amendments have been added in subsequent years providing additional programs for the teaching of

---

[2] A possible exception is the Fortune Society, a voluntary organization that relies on private funding and was established in 1967 in New York City to help people who have been in jail find jobs or acquire vocational training. The Fortune Society began a tutoring program in 1974, after discovering that most of those whom it was trying to place were reading below third-grade level. Although most of its 80 volunteers are middle-class, similar to those in NALA and LVA, the paid counseling staff is made up of ex-offenders. The Fortune Society's annual budget is about $520,000, of which some $160,000 is directed to its educational program ("Questions and Answers," n.d.).

English as a second language and for adults in custodial care. The regulations permitted under the amendments allowed for greater emphasis on secondary education than in the early years of the program.

ABE is designed for adults 16 years and older who are out of school and who have not completed high school, that is, for the roughly 59 million Americans described in Chapter 2. Enrollment figures have increased over the years from about 38,000 in 1965 to an estimated 1,700,000 in 1976. Among participants in 1976, about 20 percent were learning English as a second language. Another 5 percent were adults in hospitals, correctional institutions, and other custodial facilities. About 55 percent were women. Some 35 percent were unemployed; 9 percent were receiving public assistance.[3] No figures are entirely accurate because many state and local reports are based only on administrative estimates. There is also a high likelihood of duplicate recording procedures; it is hard to determine whether students enrolled in a given program are the same ones recorded previously. Despite the inevitable tendency to show the highest possible number of "average daily attenders" to qualify for state funding, annual increases are significant.

The federal government provides funds to the 50 states and 6 territories. A base amount is allotted to each and the rest is supplied on the basis of a formula related to the number of persons 16 and over not in school. Federal funding in 1972 amounted to $51,134,000. In 1976 it was $67,500,000. State participation in the funding of programs within their own borders varies greatly. In some states all contributions come from cities, towns, counties, and other local sources. In 1976 state and local funding was about $184,000,000 (NACAE, 1977b).

While state education agencies are ultimately responsible for the administration and supervision of all ABE programs within the state—including teacher-training, curriculum selection and development, evaluation, and fiscal accountability—decentralization and local autonomy are the rules rather than the exceptions. One of the most striking impressions that we received from responses to a questionnaire we sent to state ABE directors was that state offices of education appear to be structured in much

---

[3]Unless otherwise noted, all statistics were obtained from an unpublished report prepared by the Office of Education for UNESCO and confirmed in telephone interviews, June 1978.

the same way as the federal system. Like the federal agencies, the state offices of education view themselves largely as disbursing agencies, responsible for allocating funds to individual communities. They act as conduits for funding rather than as leaders in adult basic education practice. The primary initiative for the establishment and programming of activities rests, consequently, in local hands.

One other significant administrative practice within ABE is the wide variety of cosponsorship arrangements. Poverty-related and job-training programs that are federally funded and administered by the states and local agencies often contract with local ABE administrative bodies to arrange basic education for their clients or trainees. Each program has its own pattern. Some of these federally funded programs send their constituents to regular ABE classes. Others operate programs in centers of their own or contract for ABE teachers to go into homes. Custodial institutions frequently cosponsor programs with ABE.

Employers and, sometimes, unions also cosponsor ABE programs, often on their own premises and occasionally during working hours (Mezirow et al., 1975, pp. 121–122). In general it is the larger businesses that enter into cosponsoring arrangements with ABE, chiefly to increase the language and literacy skills of minority workers. One extensive study of business attitudes and practices with reference to worker education showed that business leaders are loath to provide services they feel the schools should have provided. Only 30,000 of the employees studied were in basic education courses cosponsored by companies, while 3 million were in other courses of study on company time (Lusterman, 1976, p. 42).

A third heterogeneous group of agencies that cosponsor programs with ABE includes local churches, ethnic and poverty organizations, housing developments, self-help groups—what might be called grass-roots or community organizations.

There are many advantages and disadvantages for ABE administrators in cosponsoring programs with other agencies, but the most significant factor on the plus side seems to be the entree offered into constituency groups that might not otherwise become related to ABE programs.

ABE programs are so broad and diverse and their impact so significant, if for no other reason than the sheer size of the ABE enterprise, that we will conclude our discussion by asking some questions. The answers will help summarize the vast literature that already exists about ABE.[4] The questions are: How does ABE function locally? Who participates in ABE? Who is there to help them? What goes on in the ABE classroom? What teaching materials are used? What factors seem to inhibit success in realizing learner and program objectives?

How does ABE function locally? Broad descriptions of program goals tell us remarkably little about what happens to people in those programs and how much satisfaction they find through them.

Most of the excellent research and experimentation in ABE programs is limited to the locale where such work took place. There is little evidence that innovations spread. Fortunately, there is one study that presents a clear picture of the flavor of classroom interactions across the broad spectrum of diverse, local ABE programs. A research team conducted an extensive study of urban ABE in the public schools. They used innovative field and survey methods and produced a description of how the program functions locally, the dynamics of classroom situations, and the perspectives and characteristics of those involved. They concentrated on urban areas, where some 86 percent of the ABE programs are taking place. Their findings were published in *Last Gamble on Education* (Mezirow et al., 1975). We rely heavily on their data in our overview of ABE and recommend their rich, illustrative report to anyone who wishes to understand how this major program affects those who participate in it.

---

[4]We discovered early in our search that the literature on such topics as adult fundamental or basic education, educationally disadvantaged adults, urban adult education, rural adult education, adult literacy/illiteracy, financing of adult education, staff-training and administration, all yielded vast amounts of material on ABE. Seldom were other programs mentioned. Research, surveys, statistics, literature searches, experiments, analyses, critiques, evaluations, and opinions abound. Bibliographies of curriculum materials, reports of teacher-training workshops, descriptions of innovations in recruitment, methods, materials, policy recommendations about funding and legislation, projects designed for specific ethnic groups, "how to" guides for every aspect of local programs, studies of the age, race, and sex of participants, cost and benefit analyses—all were numerous. Since our focus is on the educationally disadvantaged themselves, we have only sampled this prolific literature related to a program which, despite its size and level of funding, reaches only a small percentage of persons with serious literacy problems. We saw no need to repeat the work of others. Furthermore, most of the material is presented from the point of view of researchers, professional educators, administrators, and policy-makers. The perceptions, views, and attitudes of clients are notably absent from the bulk of the literature.

Who participates in ABE? Even though HEW regulations initially required that no more than 20 percent of a state's allotment be spent for secondary-level instruction and that first priority be given to programs for students who had not completed fourth grade (with second priority going to those between fifth and eighth grade levels), reporting procedures did not permit the enforcement of these regulations and they were later changed to permit greater latitude. Official U.S. Office of Education statistics indicate that in 1976 only 32 percent of ABE students were enrolled at the beginning level (grades 1 through 4), 33 percent at the intermediate level (grades 5 through 8), and 35 percent at the advanced level (grades 9 through 12). About 9 percent of those enrolled in ABE in 1976 received certification at eighth grade level and 11 percent of them passed the GED tests.

In general, ABE participants are among the 60 million "targets" who are most in tune with middle-class norms and school practice (ibid., p. 54). They desire to improve their literacy skills even though life conditions of many enrollees make it difficult for them to maintain any disciplined, long-term interaction with formal institutions. The majority of students in urban programs have already spent many unprofitable years in the school system—eight, ten, even twelve years—yet their literacy problems persist (ibid., p. 39). They still believe that it is worth trying for. Racially and ethnically they reflect the population of the inner-city. Cities in which a large number of professionals and skilled workers from other countries have immigrated have proportionately more enrollees in their English as a second language section of ABE. In most cities two-thirds of ABE participants are women (ibid., p. 39).

ABE is a "creaming operation" that picks up those persons who are the most ready: unskilled laborers seeking better jobs, some unemployed young people, mothers wanting to help their children, educated aliens, and aliens without documents who are highly motivated to find a better place for themselves than they had in the societies they fled (ibid., p. 54). All these and many more take a "last gamble" on ABE.

Who is there to help them? Like every other educational enterprise, the effectiveness of local programs and classroom practices depends in large measure on the perspectives, background, and openness of teachers and other personnel who relate directly to the learners and, to a lesser degree, on the assumptions of administrators about the purposes of the program.

Many of the teachers, far greater than the proportion in the public schools, have the same racial and ethnic origins as their students. Most of the teachers are young—under 40. Three-fifths are women and 80 percent work part-time in ABE (ibid., pp. 57–58). They like working with adults—three-fifths stated that teaching adults is personally more rewarding than teaching children (ibid., p. 63). Black teachers and those in English as a second language put more emphasis on including functional content than do other teachers. There is some indication that black teachers show higher student retention rates than white teachers (ibid., pp. 26, 28). In short, the teachers are as varied as their students. Age, years of experience, type of program and class taught, and degree of administrative support all condition how teachers act and react.

What goes on in the ABE classroom? Most classes are taught in traditional elementary school teaching styles. Exceptions, however, are also numerous. Intensive efforts to reward success and minimize failure provide a certain amount of freedom for students to proceed at their own paces, and a relaxed classroom atmosphere often permits students to come and go as they please (ibid., pp. 16–32).

Some teachers exhibit great skill in appropriate uses of instruction on individual, group, and class levels, offering a loosely structured approach. Others have made effective use of new instructional technologies through learning laboratories, programmed instruction, and educational television. Mobile learning units and "armchair instruction," that is, a combination of indigenous recruiters, home instruction, and counseling, have been important in some areas in encouraging learners to go into regular ABE classes, seek job training, or enroll in high school equivalency programs (ibid., pp. 22–25). Since 1973 the ABE program in Vermont has pioneered both in the use of full-time, paid home tutors and literacy volunteers and by involving new groups and community members of all ages. Vermont received special recognition in the 1976 Literacy Day Activities.[5]

What teaching materials are used? A variety of commercially prepared texts and workbooks for basic skills and English language skills are used in most classes. These are sometimes in short supply and often teachers are forced to fall back on more easily available materials written for children. Materials pub-

---

[5]Information based on a report in World Education files.

lished by Laubach's New Readers' Press and by the *Reader's Digest* are popular, but there are many other texts arranged around reading, writing, spelling, and arithmetic drill. The American Library Association and Literacy Volunteers of America have prepared excellent annotated bibliographies based on careful evaluation of the most commonly used materials.

While teachers are almost universally encouraged to prepare their own materials relevant to the learners' lives, little time is actually allotted for such efforts (ibid., p. 26). Experimental workshops on the use of the newspaper as a learning tool for basic education have been conducted in several states.

Student achievement seems to be higher when maximum use is made of materials prepared by the students themselves or by the teachers working closely with them and lower when commercially prepared materials are used. A combination of commercial and student-developed materials may yield the best results of all. In one center that reported a high level of student achievement, participants wrote group stories, songs, and poems. Sentences were first written on the blackboard and later typed, illustrated, and distributed to other centers in the program[6] (*A Guide to Using Language Experience,* 1973; Harman, 1974; *Quitman County Center,* 1970).

What factors seem to inhibit success in realizing learner and program objectives? Poor attendance seems to haunt ABE. Forty percent of the teachers questioned indicated that irregular attendance was their most difficult problem (Mezirow et al., p. 67). The mix of students, absenteeism, and turn-over are, in the teachers' opinion, the most serious obstacles to learning and teaching. The fear of losing students and thereby jeopardizing funding sometimes leads to greater attention to recording attendance than to educational practice. It also has a heavy influence—whether for good or ill—on classroom norms about conduct, freedom of

---

[6]In 1973 the U.S. Office of Education invited World Education to create teacher- and learner-generated materials. The result was a project called the apperception-interaction method (AIM). Teachers prepare simple, open-ended stories based on experiences and problem situations related to them by their students. Accompanying photographs are used to start discussion. The AIM stories serve both as reading material for the learners and, also, as a way to focus their thoughts on specific, everyday problems. In addition to stimulating student interest and involvement, the AIM process and others based on locally generated materials assist teachers whose cultural and educational backgrounds are different from their students to better understand the needs of those with whom they work (Brehmer, 1977).

arrival and leaving times, and the ability to join classes at any stage in their progress (ibid., pp. 73–76).

Closely related to these problems is the drop-out rate. About one-third of those who enroll in ABE do not complete their courses, which generally last for a semester. Changes in job status (getting or losing a job or moving to a better one), health problems, difficulties in finding and arranging childcare, family demands, inconvenient class schedules, lack of interest, and poor student-teacher relations have all been listed as reasons for abandoning courses. There are, however, few procedures for obtaining reliable feedback from drop-outs about their reactions to a program (ibid., p. 154).

The drop-out rate seems to be related to income level. One out of five of all adult education courses taken by persons with incomes under $4,000 a year is dropped; and one out of seven courses taken by persons from households with incomes between $4,000 and $6,000 is dropped. Persons whose income is in the upper ranges ($10,000 to $25,000 a year), however, are reported as dropping fewer than one out of 15 courses in which they enroll (Froomkin, 1977, p. 17). The inference is that adult education programs do not, for whatever reasons, meet the needs of the poor as well as they meet the needs of the less poor and relatively affluent.

A possible contributing factor to the failure of some students to relate well to the program is the inability of teachers and counselors—because of program expectations and time constraints—to become involved in the students' out-of-school problems or to offer continuing personal help in crises (Mezirow et al., 1975, pp. 77 and 29–30). Further many teachers are unfamiliar with the ghetto and poverty. They simply do not know the realities of the lives of their students, either the positive or oppressive aspects. A few teacher-training programs have been devised to counteract this, but, by and large, teachers are merely "told" about poverty and are offered no real-life experiences to assist their understanding.

The lack of adequate teacher-training frustrates good teaching efforts. Before 1974, funds for teacher-training and for experimentation were administered by the Office of Education. Since then, however, all these funds have been distributed by the states, with, in the opinion of many, a resulting decrease in the effectiveness of both training and experimental activities. The discretionary funds are allocated on a project-grant basis and thus are not part of any overall plan for equipping teachers. There is no formal exchange among the various states. Within regions there may be duplication of training efforts, or even no training programs at all.

Teaching adults in general and ABE students in particular is a new and uncertain profession. Funding, especially in programs cosponsored by manpower and poverty programs, is never guaranteed. In addition, inner-city programs have the disadvantage of being located in what are seen by many teachers from outside the inner-city as unsafe areas. Since classes are generally held at night, this factor assumes added importance.

The administration of funds for innovative and experimental activities by the states has resulted in what some call "56 little offices of education," with the consequent loss of any systematic, centralized attention to the evaluation of new practices and the dissemination of significant findings. For example, lack of coordination with any but the basic education activities of other government programs has resulted in ABE teachers' not knowing about valuable workshops and training conferences sponsored by regional agencies (GAO Report, 1975, p. 18).

Right to Read

Right to Read is a federally funded program that began operating in 1971. Its announced goal was to overcome illiteracy in the United States within ten years. It was intended to serve as a catalyst, stimulating efforts by states through their education agencies and private sector efforts to improve reading skills "for *all* people." Two programs under Right to Read focus on the needs of adults; community-based programs for those 16 and over, and Reading Academies. Some $5 million was distributed among about 80 Reading Academies in 1976.

A careful study of 11 community-based Right to Read projects in California corroborates informal data we collected elsewhere. Within its adult programs, considerable use was made of tutors for those beginning to read at the most basic level. Participants in most respects were similar to those who enter ABE in race, sex, and age distributions. As in ABE more teachers came from minority backgrounds than in the public schools, but fewer than the percentages of students from these groups. Teachers displayed great enthusiasm for their work, and dedication to their students. The teachers in these community-based Right to Read programs had fewer credentials than Right to Read teachers in projects involving youth or children (*Evaluation of Community-Based Right to Read Programs*, 1974, pp. 121–133).

Two other specific findings from the California study confirm experience elsewhere. First, among students whose native language was not English, those who were literate in their own language progressed faster and showed higher retention rates. Second, those who had been referred to the program by counselors achieved less than those who had come hoping to realize personal objectives.

To assess Right to Read in terms of its own goal, the eradication of illiteracy, leads inevitably to the conclusion that the goal itself is unrealistic. David Olson (1975), of the Ontario Institute for Studies in Education, has written a critique of *Toward a Literate Society* (Carroll and Chall, 1975), a series of papers commissioned by the Committee on Reading of the National Academy of Education. He describes the unfounded expectations created by the popular myth that literacy is the most significant criterion of the civilized person or society. Olson questions whether Right to Read could ever make adults already by-passed by the school system literate and whether it should even try to do so. His conclusion is that a program like Right to Read can, at the most, produce limited research, improve reading levels to a modest degree, and stimulate pilot reading programs. It has, in fact, been along these lines that Right to Read has made its most valuable contributions.

Prisons and Other Correctional Institutions

Almost every known agency in the United States that provides conventional literacy education offers programs within prisons and other correctional facilities. One out of every 14 ABE participants in 1971 was in a program run in a prison. Why? There are relatively few recruiting problems in prisons. The involuntarily stable population is less affected by family and work demands, and attends more consistently. This tends to make prisoners particularly promising students, especially for agencies whose funding is determined by numbers enrolled.

The voluntary literacy organizations cooperate with government programs by supplying trained community tutors. Right to Read, the Comprehensive Employment and Training Act (CETA), the Veterans Administration, and the American Bar Association's Commission on Corrections all provide conventional literacy training in correctional institutions, and in some cases relate that skill to job-training programs. We found no research on the relation between basic education courses in prisons and the successful rehabilitation of prisoners. The literature does contain some case studies of individuals who discovered their own intellectual aptitudes for the first time in prison, some of them moving rapidly through stages of schooling and eventually winning advanced degrees. The Fortune Society provides examples of the success of basic education and tutoring for ex-offenders ("Questions and Answers," n.d.).

Libraries

"Here we sit in this enormous, beautiful building. Every day we suffer financial cuts which affect our program capability. Out there, all around us, are people who desperately need free, reliable information. They don't know we are here. We don't know how to reach them. For too long we didn't even try to reach them. Now I wonder if we are going to die as a viable institution before they and we discover each other." So spoke an official of the Brooklyn Public Library. He went on to describe some of the federally and state-funded programs the Brooklyn Public Library has inaugurated, commenting that, in too many instances, it has to mount programs that fit funding categories rather than follow initiatives out of its growing awareness of needed community services.

Do libraries simply exist for those who seek their services or do they have a responsibility to reach out into the community? The American Library Association sought answers to this question in 1963 with the establishment of a standing committee on reading improvement for adults. Understandably, attention was initially focused on serving those without conventional literacy skills. Tutoring services and classes were established. Literacy Volunteers of America had done some excellent tutoring and small-group work in reading within libraries. A series of joint library and community projects, cited in a report on literacy activities published in 1966 (MacDonald, 1966), includes some interesting initiatives involving libraries and such programs as Aid to Dependent Children (programs for mothers), public media programs, Right to Read, PTAs, church and civic groups, home demonstration and farm agents, and health and welfare agencies. Many of the initiatives were headed by local voluntary citizen groups.

In 1973 the Appalachian Adult Education Center (AAEC) published a far more radical examination of the role of libraries in basic education activities. The AAEC observed that, before an institution can render effective service, it must see itself as a service institution. The report sees both the library and public school as resisting the changes in concept and organization necessary to serve disadvantaged adults. Attitudes of professionals and of supporting boards of directors, fiscal systems, and staff-training methods combine to prevent spontaneous change. Even such simple barriers as preferring to provide books because they are easier to manage than pamphlets, assume great significance in determining whether libraries are able to step into the world of 59 million potential clients who have not always found them helpful in the past (*Interrelating Library and Basic Education Services*, 1973).

The AAEC offers four possible models, as well as an extensive bibliography, to assist communities in which there is interest in combining library services with those of other agencies. AAEC has also developed a handbook listing materials that people with reading difficulties and information needs can actually use—books, pamphlets, films, records, games, and cassette tapes, all of which are identified as to source, reading level, and cost (Gotsick, et al., 1976). The AAEC report concludes that, although the need for the planning, coordination, and routine delivery of the broad range of services that libraries could offer is great and has been frequently discussed, the initiative to do so has not yet been taken.

Summary: Category 1 Programs

Those who rely chiefly on statistical data to indicate either achievement or impact will find little that is conclusive about the conventional literacy programs we have just considered. Some 27,000 reading tutors—a rough estimate—have worked in one-to-one relationships in the last year. Perhaps 100,000 in prisons and other correctional institutions were reached either by tutoring or in classes, and some of those would be included in the 27,000 mentioned above. No overall figures for those reached by library programs are available. The total ABE population, which includes most of those in correctional institutions, accounts for the largest number in public and cosponsored classes for educationally disadvantaged adults: anywhere from 1.7 to 3 million, or from 2 to 4.5 percent of the "target" population of 54 to 64 million (NACAE, 1977b). The ABE figures include adults working below the eighth grade level, those at the secondary school level, those working on preparation for the general equivalency diploma, and persons studying English as a second language. Impact studies and solid evaluations are even scarcer than accurate reports of the numbers of participants.

From the point of view of the learner, however, some progress is evident. ABE is only nine years old. Before it existed there was no basic instruction generally available for those who sought help. A plan for major evaluation of the first nine years is already approved and awaits funding (NACAE, 1977b). Meanwhile, such studies as Mezirow's point clearly to several areas in which immediate initiatives would substantially improve the quality of instruction and perhaps increase retention rates.

Although the numbers of students reached are not large in relation to the need, teachers and counselors play a significant role by encouraging and supporting the fearful, providing resource information to those intimidated by oppressive bureaucracies, and responding with sensitivity to students' personal dilemmas. The hard-core poor need these human links to embark on any program.

COMPETENCY-BASED PROGRAMS: CATEGORY 2

In recent years many adult educators have moved away from reliance on external institutions and toward individual autonomy and self-selected learning objectives. Educators around the world are increasingly defining education as a life-long process with recurrent access to educational services. One of the educational goals of this movement is to shift responsibility for the pursuit of learning to the individual (Broschart, 1976; Gardner, 1961).

Our definitions of conventional and functional literacy reflect this view of education as it applies to those who society sees as "undereducated." The provision of diversified opportunities, individualized resources, and teaching-learning modes for those who have dropped out or were pushed out of traditional schooling are significant recent developments.

Those who plan education programs based on the existing competencies of people look first at what the adult has already learned. They are less interested in whether the new competencies sought by learners have utility within the educational system itself than in whether these competencies are important in the person's life. They encourage people to learn what they need to know rather than simply to pass examinations. Decisions about scheduling, locations for learning, teacher qualification, and materials are all being reexamined from the point of view of the learners' desired outcomes. Thus, for example, the regional centers for community education affiliated with the National Center for Community Education are trying to apply learning to solving problems, to draw upon the services, resources, and educational forces of the community, and to accommodate students of all ages at a variety of times and places. They are basing education on the cultural traditions of the community and trying to help all the people of the community to judge what they can or want to learn and to discover how to do so (*Centers for Community Education Development*, 1975).

The competency-based approaches have influenced more traditional programs. In many states ABE teachers now receive training that stresses the use of community resources, solving problems, and how their work in class is related to the lives and needs of their students. Funds for research and experimentation distributed by the individual states have been channeled into curriculum-development projects influenced by the findings of the Texas study of Adult Performance Levels (APL). Most of the projects are small and unrelated to each other. The U.S. Office of Education and what remains of the APL staff now employed by the Texas States Board of Education, as well as individuals, schools of education, and others influenced by APL, attempt to make an impact on ABE by moral suasion through conferences and workshops and by disseminating information about successful models based on APL (*Competency-Based Adult Education Report*, 1976 and *Competency-Based Adult Education Profiles*, 1976).

Competency-based education describes an approach that places the skills and competencies needed by the learner for life—either personal or job-related—above those required by schools or other educational institutions.[7] The increased attention to functional skills and competencies has also resulted in new programs. Some of these will be described below.

Our discussion of selected job-related or competency-based programs (category 2) focuses on five locales for such programs:

---

[7]We have not included the programs of federal agencies other than those of HEW. Manpower and poverty programs offer a wide range of job training programs in addition to contracting with ABE for basic education classes. These are within the scope of this report and inclusive consideration of functional literacy programs should include them. Unfortunately, however, the constraints within which we worked prevented us from including them. Most of these programs suffer from the same restrictions that affect the more narrowly defined educational programs; that is, long-term effects depend on basic changes in social and economic structures and the values [and goals] that sustain them. This is clear from the cutbacks that these programs suffer in any period of economic recession.

the military, labor unions, the New York State Division for Youth, cultural and ethnic organizations, and other community-based programs. These locales are obviously neither mutually exclusive nor totally inclusive, but they do provide a convenient set of pegs for our survey of an extremely diverse program category.

The Military

As in other parts of the world, the military in the United States has a stake in adult literacy. The U.S. Navy recently reported that its recruiting efforts are seriously hampered by literacy deficiencies among potential enlistees. The executive officer of the Navy recruiting district in Detroit recently stated, "Only one recruit out of 10 passes our test, and the basic reason is they have difficulty reading and understanding the words." In response to this situation, the Navy has begun a remedial reading program for those who read below the sixth grade level, but acknowledges that the program, which lasts only four to six weeks, has had only fair success—not surprising given what is already known about the limitations of such courses. Most programs devised by the military to answer its needs have been similar, discrete, limited-literacy training courses, but the armed services have undertaken some innovative and illuminating programming and research (Weintraub, 1977).

The Department of Defense has been highly praised for programs conducted within the armed forces aimed at reducing the illiteracy encountered among recruits during World War II. One observer called them the most sophisticated education delivery system in the country, with supporting research and development unknown or unused elsewhere (Broschart, 1976). Unfortunately for those who might wish to learn from these efforts and apply their findings, the whole program seems to have come to a halt with the discontinuance of the draft.

In the 1950s and 1960s programs were undertaken for increasing employment opportunities of poor and minority personnel within the military service. Many of these programs had a basic literacy component as well as training in functional skills for jobs that had civilian counterparts. Impressive results were recorded in the preliminary pilot programs for the first 5,000 to 10,000 men. Then support for these programs diminished and finally disappeared. One author reports a conversation with persons in the Public Affairs Office, Department of Defense, who stated rather baldly: "Now we need a smaller number of talented people. We do not need, nor do we have the resources, to recruit and educate and then train illiterates'' (Ryan and Furlong, 1975, p. 179).

Project REALISTIC attempted to discover the reading demands of various occupational specialties within the Army and to learn whether standardized reading tests were helpful in predicting job success (Sticht et al., 1972). Perhaps, it was posited, literacy and educational levels that were stated as requirements for certain jobs were unnecessarily high. Indeed, this turned out to be true. Sticht comments on the absence in the Army of job-related developmental reading materials and sequenced job reading tasks related to the literacy programs. Apparently, relatively short periods of literacy training resulted in improvement in reading ability, but, without reinforcement in later phases of training, the improvement was likely to be comparatively short-lived (Sticht et al., 1973).

We mention the military programs for two reasons. First, there is a general belief that they were unusually good conventional and functional literacy training programs. Second, the programs were carefully studied and that research should not be forgotten but, rather, built upon. The fact that there is no draft at present does not greatly reduce the need for the military to continue and even expand its efforts in the field of literacy training.

Labor Unions

Certain labor unions,[8] in addition to cosponsoring ABE programs with management, business, and industry, have developed programs of their own in response to the specific needs of their members, many of whom have a first language other than English, possess minimal literacy skills, and are unaware of their civic rights and privileges. (The unions themselves may not necessarily classify all these endeavors as educational, at least not in the same sense as ABE or basic literacy training.)

Most unions—60 to 70 percent—offer courses to acquaint their members with collective bargaining and grievance procedures. They also offer basic orientation in politics and economics. For example, in the Seaman's International Union's school at Piney Point, Maryland, most students start out unable to read and write. The claim is made that they all learn to read through studying their union's constitution, working on a newsletter, and using other innovative methods rooted in their needs as seamen.

Local 3 of the International Brotherhood of Electrical Workers

---

[8]Data and examples for this section are all from The Labor Education Center, Rutgers University, supplied by Edgar Lee Rosenthal in July 1977.

(IBEW) increases the skills of many of its members by training them to be basic education teachers to fellow members of the union. It also runs seminars on human values, racism, and other civic matters, makes available thousands of tickets to cultural events, and encourages the use of museums, libraries, and other community institutions.

One local of the Laborers' International Union has experimented with mobile education units, which carry the classroom to the work sites of members, especially immigrant workers learning English. The women who hand out paychecks act as recruiters for the program. Another local has successfully negotiated paid educational leaves for its workers and administers these together with management. The union encourages its workers to take advantage of these leaves by providing tutoring services for those who need literacy and language skills before they can take part. An information program helps workers, most of whom are women, to understand how the leaves are linked to guaranteed jobs and benefits. The educational leave may lead to jobs in different fields with higher status; a nurse's helper, for instance, may study nursing or a kitchen worker may study to become a dental assistant.

Craft unions, among others, run apprenticeship programs combining schooling with on-the-job learning from a master craftsman. Remedial literacy, language, and computation are offered in the context of the particular job training.

Those familiar with these union programs claim that their members learn more rapidly and with greater satisfaction when they are able to learn in preparation for specific jobs, at the work site, or in schools run by the unions for union members.

New York State Division for Youth

New York State's Division for Youth (DFY) has taken the lead in exploring how education can become meaningful "to the many turned off and dropped out youth who, at best, see education as irrelevant to them and their lives, and who, at worst, harbor deep resentments and hostilities toward school, teachers, and administrators. How can attitudes that have been developing for many years be changed? How can education play a vital role in the rehabilitative process?" (DFY staff memo, Dec. 31, 1976).

The DFY works with young adults alienated from the conventional learning environment who have been assigned to the Division through the court system.[9] Many of them have learning

---

[9]Subsequent DFY descriptions are based on memos in World Education files.

disabilities. All are at loggerheads with their environment; they "lack academic and vocational skills and competencies, lack self-awareness and self-understanding, have negative self-concepts . . . are not goal-oriented . . . lack problem-solving skills, exhibit antisocial behaviors . . . have uncertainty and anxiety about their role or place in their environment." Administrators who must design educational and rehabilitation programs for these young people face difficult problems.

The DFY has concluded that traditional school methods and procedures have not been and will not be effective with the youth with whom they work. In 1977, DFY inaugurated a new system based on comprehensive, individual assessments of needs and the provision of opportunities for self-planned learning to meet personal and vocational objectives. This includes a basic curriculum around specified objectives: mastery of basic skills in communication and computation applied to reasoning and logic; ability to sort and manage knowledge (of self, community, science, history); ability to manage self and life; and ability to plan and implement action leading to personal life goals, including employment and use of leisure.

Conversations with the DFY staff revealed an urgency about the need for programs of functional education for young adults, an urgency repeated in many other locations. Horace W. Morris of the New York Urban League described these young adults:

> Their eyes are bleak. Some, strutting down the street, speak with false bravado. Others stand listlessly on street corners speaking in monotones of what they think being an adult is like. Most can barely read or write. They are 17 to 22 years old. The majority of them are minority youngsters. They are a lost generation. . . . Their lives have been programmed for emptiness (Morris, 1977).

Cultural and Ethnic Organizations

We will look briefly at the work of a few representative community-based organizations. Their programs are frequently not labeled as education. The forms are influenced less by educational theories than by the demands growing out of their minority status within a social and cultural environment different from their own. Such programs exist among Native Americans, Chicanos, blacks, welfare mothers, particular groups of Hispanic people, migrant workers, fishermen, and a host of other people whose needs draw them together within the communities in which they live and work. Much of the impetus for recent efforts grew out of the civil rights movement and from subsequent attention to the importance of group and individual pride and its potential power to improve lives restricted by social or economic injustice.

Native American Survival Schools. These schools are dedicated to teaching Native American culture and history to both children and adults. They seek to teach "what is not taught in the public schools" about Native American traditions, about treaties, about cooperative ways of living, and in doing so to develop their own community leaders. The names of these survival schools indicate something of the spirit that moves them: "We Shall Survive," and "Heart of the Earth." There is ample testimony of participants moving from despair to the acquisition of new skills and significant self-confidence. A conscious effort is made to encourage previously unmotivated students to learn skills that give them the option of getting along in the larger society and to understand the relationship between the demands of the two quite different ways of life (*Survival School System*, 1974; *Heart of the Earth Survival School*, 1976).

The Barrio Education Project. This program serves the Chicano community of San Antonio, Texas. Initial efforts to meet the needs of expectant parents through childbirth-preparation classes have resulted in a completely different relationship between the Mexican-American community and the health delivery services of the area. Out of this have come literacy classes in Spanish to enable the speaker of Spanish to affirm a unique cultural heritage and, out of that heritage, to build a positive community self-image. Teaching methods have developed from interviews and conversations with inhabitants of the several barrios within which the BEP operates. Concerns revealed in this process result not only in materials for learning but also in initiatives to consolidate political and economic rights and to produce community change. The use of art as a medium of communication has revealed talents of which individuals can be proud and also helped to discover messages that illiterates want to deliver about themselves and their aspirations (Barrio Education Project, n.d.).

Southern Christian Leadership Conference (SCLC) Citizenship Education Schools. One of the most remarkable stories in the field of adult basic education resulted from the vision, commitment, and creative educational approaches of one black woman, Septima Clark. Impelled by her confidence in her own people and by her conviction that they must become full participants in the life of the South, from which they had been excluded for so long, she began what eventually became a major program in 11 states of the Deep South. The program ran from 1957 to 1970. She was joined in her early organizing efforts by Esau Jenkins and by persons associated with the Highlander Folk School (Clark, 1962).

Their first Citizenship Education School was on John's Island, off the coast of Georgia. Early on they realized that outsiders, even black leaders from the SCLC, would have difficulty reaching people in the rural communities, where the work was most needed. They trained persons from these communities, many of them women, who, although they had little or no formal education, displayed leadership and teaching skills. As long as the trainees themselves could read and speak to others without embarrassment, they could become teachers of their neighbors.

Training sessions for the teachers were held in Liberty County, Georgia. Buses came from as far west as eastern Texas and as far north as northern Virginia. The Election Law became the reading text, because one of the ultimate goals was that all the students should become registered voters. The curriculum, however, developed by those who worked in the program, included all the areas of daily life: good farming methods, homemaking, health, nutrition, taxes, and the duties and rights of citizens. Teachers were paid $30 a month. Each worked with about 12 learners in kitchens, beauty parlors, community buildings, living rooms, and the out-of-doors—wherever space could be found where people were free to gather. Some 200 schools were established.

A grant of $250,000 from the Field Foundation made it possible for SCLC to undertake the program. The program was discontinued after Septima Clark's retirement and the death of Martin Luther King, Jr., but some interesting activities resulted. The Esau Jenkins Memorial Scholarship Fund was established and continues to grow. It makes grants to black high school students to enable them to go on to college. As recently as July 1977, Septima Clark Experimental School was founded in Charleston on the same principles and approaches as the Citizenship Education Schools (Burch, 1977).

In response to the need of organizations and institutions working at the community level for communication, resource development, information dissemination, technical assistance, and relevant research, a new agency has been created. Founded in

1976 with major support from the Fund for the Improvement of Postsecondary Education (FIPSE), the Clearinghouse for Community Based Free Standing Educational Institutions is a nonprofit national membership organization of community based and controlled institutions. Members of the Clearinghouse include both institutions offering alternative forms of higher education and community organizations.

The Clearinghouse defines community based education as a process that provides meaningful learning based on experiences rooted in the life, environment, culture, and aspirations of the learner. Clearinghouse members see the empowerment of the community as a natural consequence of this process since the analysis of needs, the fostering of critical awareness of the environment and the forces affecting it, the ability to reach decisions and to act responsibly on them, and the use of tools and resources from within the community are all stressed as part both of education and of healthy individual and community growth.

Some of the community education and development organizations that are members of the Clearinghouse include: the Barrio Education Project (San Antonio), East Harlem Block Schools (New York), the Experimental and Bilingual Institute (New York), Native American Educational Services (Chicago), Home Education Livelihood Program (Albuquerque), Solidaridad Humana (New York), and the Federation of Southern Cooperatives (Epes, Alabama).

The members of the Clearinghouse constantly face a challenge from more traditional institutions. Recognition and legitimacy within the academic community impose evaluation criteria that, if too narrowly followed, can cause the erosion of the community base that is the very source of the effectiveness of these new educational organizations.

Museums and galleries. Museums and art galleries have traditionally been passive transmitters of culture and have been oriented to the educationally elite. They are preservers of what has already been, not agents of change. In recent years, however, some have taken more active roles. Courses in filmmaking and the visual arts began the process. Those who looked toward a vocation or avocation in the arts became involved in museum and gallery activities. More recently, museums have begun to make available information and educational opportunities about the cultural roots of particular segments of the population—Native Americans, blacks, Hispanic people. Museums with general programs have arranged special and widely publicized exhibits. New museums have come into being with cultural foci as their chief concern.

A network of museums specializing in black history and cultural traditions is now spread across the country and has regular conferences for directors and administrators to enable them to gain skills both in fund-raising and in new methods of community service, education, and relationships. One of the museum directors with whom we talked is creating a center for education called the Weeksville Project in the Bedford-Stuyvesant area of Brooklyn (*Society for the Preservation of Weeksville*, n.d.).

Weeksville was a free black community from about 1825 to 1875. When facts came to light about the existence of this community, some citizens tried to trace that early history. An organization was formed with the goal of discovering and preserving the documents and artifacts of the culture of the area now known as Bedford-Stuyvesant. They have bought three historic houses and in them will eventually establish a museum. The educational theory that underlies Weeksville and similar projects is that, as a people comes to know that it has a history of which it can be proud, it also develops an incentive to learn more about itself and its heritage, to build its present and future, and to gain positive skills that enable active participation in society.

For our purposes, it is interesting to note the educational effect this project has had as a basis for speculation about the potential power of all such projects. A broad cross-section of community residents, including schoolchildren, parents, Boy Scouts, college students, teachers, housewives, and senior citizens, has participated in the project in a variety of ways, including digging for artifacts at the site of a block of houses torn down to make way for a housing development. Attics of long-time residents have yielded photographs and books. One of the prize finds was a tintype of an unknown woman; the picture so impresses those who see it that the search for information goes on. Schoolchildren and their parents have already become caught up in the project, and their attitude toward themselves and their community has changed noticeably. A doctoral thesis has been written on this search, detailing some of the positive educational and social benefits of the living project for those involved (Thompson, 1977).

Other Community-Based Programs

Leadership and administration for the projects described in this section come from within the community served. They are organized around community objectives relevant to the quality of life of the participants. Groups may be ongoing, with new agenda developing naturally from issues of lively concern.

Civic Literacy. Many burgeoning projects are devoted to regaining for citizens some control over the institutions and life of their communities—schools, health services, environment, recreational facilities, public transportation systems, and many others. While some of these endeavors are apparently controlled by middle-class citizens, increasing efforts are made to include representation from the whole community. The Syracuse Civic Literacy Project, sponsored by Syracuse University, for example has tried to include a cross-section of the population in its workshops. (Its realization leaves much to be desired, however; the print orientation of the workshops has been an inhibiting factor for many.) As in the indigenous projects described earlier, participants have gained new insights into their educational needs (Ziegler, 1974).

Similar initiatives have been undertaken in Philadelphia, Dallas, Washington, D.C., and other cities. Some organizers of these projects have difficulty letting the citizens determine the movement from one area of concern to another and designing action around the interrelationship of the issues. There is always a temptation to center activities around the issues perceived by the smaller group who initially conceived the project (Theobald, 1976).

Neighborhood houses and social service agencies. The best neighborhood houses and social service agencies have developed community-based programs. Although trustees and boards of these agencies generally come from outside the community, effective agencies today tend to select their administrative and leadership staff from their own neighborhoods or from similar urban areas. They are also moving from individual casework and counseling to group work rooted in the communities in which they exist.

Henry Street Settlement House/Urban Life Center in New York City has adopted this approach.[10] The Parent-Child Dis-

---

[10]World Education has worked with the Henry Street staff in a two-phased leadership-education project that illustrates this action-education orientation. In the first phase, youth leaders participated in an in-service training project using a range of learner-centered methods and team approaches that they later adapted for their own work with young people. In the second phase, they used videotapes to analyze group behavior and participant needs. The videotapes became the basis for developing skills in planning and problem-solving (reports in World Education files).

covery Program, which existed at Henry Street from October 1974 to October 1977 and was patterned after the Mother-Child Home Program developed by Dr. Phyllis Levenstein of Freeport, New York, tried to reach adults through their concern for the development of their children. Trained staff went into homes whose families had children about 18 months old. They took a series of toys and books, planned to become increasingly complex as the child grew. These visits were made twice a week, for a half an hour each visit, over two years. The goal was to transfer to the parents the ability to use the toys and books to stimulate the child's growth and discovery abilities.

Many of the parents were not literate or at least not literate in English. Their hesitancy with books was overcome by helping them to use the books through "reading" from the pictures. The mothers often decided they wanted to learn to read and were given guidance to discover literacy resources for themselves. This helped them to see books as something to be enjoyed. The staff of the program become trusted friends who were able to counsel the mothers about a variety of family issues and to refer them to other services.

An important goal of the program was to stimulate parents to feel that they have some power to influence the kind of education their children would be receiving in the public schools. Group meetings for parents focused on this as well as other topics. Records are maintained on the families who were in the program to see if their children perform better in school than other children.

Among the program's liabilities were that some parents, seeing the progress their children made, wanted to push them ahead in school. Because of the books and toys left by the visitors, some of the children see the program only as a source of presents and approach adults as givers of goodies. Aware of these problems, however, staff members believed they learned to cope with them, and that the program's benefits far exceeded its liabilities (World Education files, based on interview notes).

External high school diploma programs. Our attention in this study has focused chiefly on the most disadvantaged—those with the least education, the highest unemployment, and suffering the greatest discrimination. These are the hard-to-reach persons, "the stationary poor" who have, theoretically, the highest priority in ABE programs. We have also mentioned persons who are working within ABE for high school diplomas or equivalency certificates. For many this route is long and arduous. Their options vary from one state to another, but generally include three: passing examinations to receive a high school equivalency certificate; completing an adult high school program, generally at night, for a diploma; or fulfilling alternative requirements, such as successfully completing a certain number of credit hours in a junior or community college. All three routes are academically oriented and give little explicit recognition and no academic credit for the skills acquired in adult life.

New York was the first state to recognize the existence of persons within the total population of high school dropouts who, although they feel their lack of high school credentials as a constant source of humiliation and a reminder of something left undone, nevertheless function well, lead rewarding lives, hold responsible jobs, and contribute to their communities. They may be psychologically inhibited and suffer economically in job status and mobility, and may not be eligible for further formal education. Although they appear in the statistics of the educationally disadvantaged—that is, those who have not completed high school— in no way can they be considered functionally illiterate. They are highly motivated to learn and may have succeeded in teaching themselves many competencies that those with traditional credentials do not possess. It was in recognition of these facts that the Central New York External High School Diploma Program came into being in 1973 (Nickse, 1975a).

The program recognizes and rewards what adults can do on the basis of their life experiences as mature persons, parents, workers, and active members of the local community. We will mention briefly some of the essential elements that make this an educational breakthrough not only in relation to its own specific goals but as a model for other areas of adult education. The initiative grew out of the experience of the Regional Learning Service of Central New York (RLS) in counseling adults about community learning opportunities (RLS is administering the program during its experimental phase).

Several other states are modeling projects on the New York plan. Texas has ten pilot projects; Illinois, Massachusetts, New Jersey, Oregon, and Ohio are in various stages of developing similar programs. New York State has opened five additional sites.

The external high school diploma recognizes performance in both basic skill areas (math and reading) and in "life skills" (consumer, scientific, citizenship and health awareness, and occupational preparedness); it rewards advanced occupational/vocational, academic, and specialized skills. To complete the first part of the program, the adult must pass five tests designed to elicit the person's performance in 64 designated "life-skill" competencies. The tests are flexible: three are take-home tests and two are oral. The student receives continuous feedback on progress. In the second part of the diploma assessment program, the candidate demonstrates occupational/vocational skills, advanced academic skills, or specialized skills in community organization, in art, or in music. Evidence of a year's successful employment or of certain current New York State occupational licenses may be substituted for the occupational/vocational requirement. Admissions directors of local colleges developed criteria for evidence of advanced academic skills. The candidates present a portfolio containing information about their educational objectives and evidence of their ability to do college work (Nickse, 1975a and b).

A regional committee representative of the community acts as a school board for the program. A local school diploma, no different from the diplomas awarded other high school graduates, is given at the successful completion of the requirements.

A profile study of the first 50 persons to complete the program documents their tremendous interest in and enthusiasm for learning and the remarkable number of continuing education and work-related courses they had taken over the years (Nickse, 1976). The types of jobs they hold and the variety of their community volunteer work do not fulfill any stereotypes of high school drop-outs. There must be many others similarly motivated and with similar experience in other communities. These persons fit clearly into the AAEC Group 1; they are ready to learn and are filled with hope. That they did not possess formal credentials results from pressures in their lives, early marriages, economic need, or lack of interest in high school courses. They are not academic underachievers. For them, programs that recognize their experience and abilities are essential. How many are there? No one knows.

To an outside observer immersed in the massive problems of adult basic education, some of the most significant aspects of this external diploma program emerged in interviews. The openness and flexibility of the staff responsible for the program were a breath of fresh air. The core group of personnel came from several disciplines—not only adult education. They were not tied to any specific set of assumptions, published findings, or curricula, but found gratification in changes not only in assessment procedures but in the definitions of desirable competency areas and skills. The statement of the program's first director, Ruth Nickse, that it is not "cast in concrete, but rather in Silly Putty," reflects this openness.

The words "dignity" and "recognition" occur again and again. Everyone related in any way to the project is required to see enhancing the candidate's self-confidence as a primary task. Learning consultants are *not* tutors or teachers. They work with the candidates to assist in decisions about steps to be taken, to administer the diagnostic testing, and maintain a relationship with the candidates as they work through the process to the final assessment. Forty-four percent of the first group to receive diplomas felt that some candidates, depending on the person, could go through the process without any consultant, and most felt that the learning consultant was important chiefly in the beginning of the work. In other words, the first candidates—while they appreciated the personally supportive contact provided by the consultant—felt responsible for their own achievements (Nickse, 1976).[11]

Conclusion: Competency-based and Job-related Programs

The tension between institutional goals and individual goals has been overcome in many of these programs. Participants may take advantage of what is offered because it seems appropriate to them as a way to meet their information and training needs— as in the special programs offered by labor unions, museums, and neighborhood houses—or they come together around a basic concern—health care (Barrio Education Project), voter registration (Southern Christian Leadership Conference), ethnic identity (survival schools, etc.)—and determine what they can do about a particular issue and what resources are required, including resources they need for their own learning.

Although the attempts within the military to link conventional literacy and job training apparently did not progress far enough to yield the hoped-for results, the methods that were used offer a valuable body of information for further study. We found the external high school degree program in New York takes the

---

[11]Linda Lehman-Hill, presently in charge of the assessment program, commented that subsequent candidates have been a little less motivated, a little less qualified. It may be necessary to adjust the process in the future for somewhat different candidates.

students' own life experiences seriously, and provides a useful example of what can be achieved when community resources are mobilized around a single objective.

We are dealing here not with programs that reach large numbers, but with programs whose design, methods, and intent may serve as valuable models as we look at the broader problem and seek alternative approaches to learning.

Persons involved point to several specific advantages they see in the unstructured nature of these programs:

1. The involvement of community agencies, resources, people, and institutions outside the strictly educational world.
2. Their focus on individual assessment of interest and need, and their appreciation of the background of participants.
3. The pressure (from students and the situation itself) to invent methods, materials, approaches, and linkages broader than anything that already exists.
4. Their emphasis on outcome criteria and measures that allow learners to start wherever they are and to move at their own pace toward meaningful objectives.

BROADCAST MEDIA—RADIO AND TELEVISION: CATEGORY 3

In our study of broadcast media as a system for the delivery of educational services to disadvantaged adults, we encountered far more material about the media's potential than we did evaluations of actual programs. Studies and proposals were numerous and imaginative. Yet the obstacles to their realization are formidable. With a few exceptions, nothing has yet been undertaken in the United States on the scale proposed by those who see in radio and television the most practical delivery system for reaching millions (*a Handbook for ETV Utilization in Adult Education*, 1975; *Korf*, 1976; *Open Education for the People*, 1976; *Public Broadcasting and Education*, 1975).

We were already familiar with several innovative programs using radio in Third World countries, most on them tied into effective tutoring and small-group work. In rural areas where radio is the most consistent link with life outside the immediate community, audiences have been large and results significant. A UNESCO survey of the use of radio and television in achieving literacy describes programs throughout the world (Maddison, 1971).[12]

In the United States and other industrialized countries, radio has served as a medium for the recruitment of students rather than as a means of instruction. Television has more frequently been used as a teaching instrument. However, because so much television programming in the United States is regional, the expense and the relatively small size of potential viewing audiences have inhibited large-scale national efforts.

We will discuss below some present program initiatives. However, an overall look at current outreach of instructional television indicates that while almost one-third of all programs on public television were "instructional in intent," less than a tenth of those programs were for adults (*Participation in Adult Education*, 1975). The percentage of broadcast hours is even smaller. And, of course, the viewing preferences of disadvantaged adults draw them to commercial rather than to public television.

Three distinct ideological and methodological approaches to the use of television in adult education are apparent: broadcast media as a means of motivation; broadcast material as a tool for discussion and assessment of learning needs of adults; and broadcast material as a medium for presenting subject matter.

Broadcast Media as a Means of Motivation

The most impelling and successful example of the use of television and radio to break down inhibitions among adults and to secure their participation in educational programs is the experience in Great Britain. The BBC took the initiative in preparing material that first appeared on television in October 1975. The high quality of the programs evoked wide interest among the general viewing public. Even fully literate persons outside the target audience were and are sufficiently interested to watch without switching off when the program comes on. Nonreaders are therefore not embarrassed to be seen watching. The British planners of the BBC program felt that it was essential to remove the stigma attached to illiteracy before any educational program could be successful; apparently they have achieved this goal.

The first program series, called *On the Move*, came on three times a week at peak viewing time. The performers were well-

---

[12]World Education has provided technical assistance to such programs in Colombia and Thailand, especially in the training of teachers and facilitators.

known television personalities. The light and appealing instructional parts were related to key words seen frequently in the everyday environment. The testimony of former nonreaders is an important aspect of each segment. At the conclusion there is information about where the viewer can get help and a phone number to call (Hargreaves, 1977).

The second series, *Your Move*, contains a larger element of instruction. Those responsible for its development benefited not only from their experience in testing and producing the earlier series, but also from the far greater willingness of nonreaders to assist and to criticize their efforts—due, it is assumed, to the progress made in overcoming the shame and stigma attached to illiteracy before *On the Move* had changed attitudes.

The most significant aspect of this massive use of broadcasting in the United Kingdom from the perspective of observers from other industrialized nations is probably the systemic support that has been provided for the program. A number of elements, at several levels and many of them interlocking, have contributed to the effectiveness of the adult literacy campaign of the United Kingdom. These include:

1. A long history of small, voluntary literacy programs.
2. The BBC initiative in television and radio programming.
3. Government funding for local projects, distributed through the newly established Adult Literacy Resource Agency (ALRA).
4. A major publicity effort through radio, newspapers, community agencies, the use of a distinctive symbol and posters, and other public efforts to recruit both learners and volunteer tutors.
5. The work of the Local Education Authorities (LEA's) in establishing programs of individual tutoring, class instruction, tutor-and teacher-training, materials development, etc.
6. The wide use of unpaid volunteers.
7. The existence of nationwide referral systems in England, Scotland, Wales, and Northern Ireland that put those who make calls to central phone numbers in touch with local programs.
8. New and varied print and broadcast materials for both teacher/tutors and learners prepared by BBC, ALRA, the British Association of Settlements, commercial publishers, and local programs, including materials developed by students themselves, said by some to be the most popular and effective.

9. The preparation by BBC of supplementary broadcast materials for presentation on radio, accompanied by student texts, to assist learners in associating the sound of spoken words with written materials (Devereux, 1977 and Stevens, 1977).

10. Extensive evaluation and research efforts coordinated by the National Institute of Adult Education (NIAE), including an assessment of the impact of the program on those involved at every level as well as action research efforts in local programs and new research on the adult learner by university centers (Jones, 1977).

We asked persons involved in each of these aspects of the plan what they would have done differently if they could start again and what they say as future developments from present experience. Replies were broad-ranging. One response, repeated several times, emphasized the need to enlarge the scope beyond conventional literacy and to involve other persons and agencies working with disadvantaged adults. Within ALRA and NIAE, concern was expressed that workers' organizations and labor unions reflect the concerns of persons who may not have reading skills as a top priority but who have educational needs that are deep-rooted and serious. They see a broader approach as a way of building on what the program has accomplished so far.

Broadcast Material as a Tool for Discussion and Assessment of Learning Needs of Adults

A quite different model includes the presentation on open broadcast of situational episodes, focused on common, daily-life problems—health, work, family, consumer affairs. In this approach, as developed by the Mississippi Authority for Educational Television, viewers learn from discussing how the characters in the dramatic episode cope with the problems. They are invited to go to adult learning centers or some other specific location if they wish to get help themselves in dealing with these and similar situations in their own lives. In this sense, the open-broadcast material also serves as motivation to encourage potential adult learners to seek help. However, the same episodes can be used at the learning center for group discussion and as practical exercises in dealing with their life situations. The episodes can also serve to pinpoint group and individual learning needs. Used in this way, the televised material becomes primarily a point of departure for classroom teachers and tutors who, through personal contact with the learners and in discussion of the materials, discover the level of need and make specific assignments. Introduction of the knowledge areas that had been determined by the Texas Adult Performance Level Study into the television episodes is integrally related to specially created materials that help the teacher to address systematically the needs of the learners.

The disciplined training of teachers to use the materials is an essential part of the Mississippi program. Teacher-training emphasizes not only the skills needed in discussing audio-visual materials, but also how to test the learners' abilities and to determine the materials and emphases needed for each learner to progress. While the development of competencies based on the Adult Performance Level is the central focus, the learner is encouraged to work on basic reading skills if those are needed. The infinite number of branching possibilities make the teachers' tasks, quite apart from the broadcast material, exceedingly difficult. So far, evaluation has been limited to the teachers' response to the episodes portrayed on television. There have been no follow-ups in actual teaching situations (*"Just Around the Corner,"* October 1975 and 1976).

The Mississippi program and others stress that the material is reusable through videocassettes, cable television, and closed-circuit broadcast. Audiocassettes are available for those who lack equipment for visual presentations. Teachers are enthusiastic because the materials provide a much-needed bridge between the classroom experience and the daily life of students. This program seems to be a prototype for a burgeoning business of producing real-life episodes to be used in teaching adults.

Questions about the materials arise at two levels. First, international experience indicates that there are other, often simpler and less-expensive teaching tools that produce the same results. In depressed urban neighborhoods and rural areas around the world, pictures, flannel-backed figures for story-telling by learners, drawings, and simple dramatizations have all been useful to spark lively exchanges of opinion among learners and to bridge the gap between teachers and students. Does televised material, designed chiefly for classroom use, contribute enough additional value to justify the considerable extra cost and the use-related difficulties? Second, is it possible for the persons involved in the sophisticated process of designing and developing televised materials to reflect accurately the impact of the issues as these are felt by poor adults and to present alternative approaches that are available within the environment in which the most disadvantaged adults actually live? Both of these questions were raised by a group of persons who work with inner-city adults after viewing several of the Mississippi cassettes.[13]

Broadcast Material as a Medium for Presenting Subject Matter

The third model presents subject matter in social studies, literature, grammar, science, mathematics, and other subjects at the level of those adults working toward the GED examinations, who are the primary audience. Some courses focus on the needs of those for whom English is a second language.

In the early 1960s a number of television programs focusing on reading improvement were developed in Memphis, Baltimore, Yakima, Washington, and Philadelphia. The Philadelphia program, *Operation Alphabet*, was widely used beyond Pennsylvania. By 1964, 100 cities had used the series distributed by the National Association for Public School Adult Education (Maddison, 1971).

Two of the most commonly used courses for high school equivalency preparation are "Your Future is Now," produced by Manpower Educational Institute of the American Foundation on Automation and Employment in New York City, and a series of 34 half-hour lessons and study guides developed and produced by Kentucky Educational Television and Cambridge Book Company. "Your Future is Now" reviews skills and concepts for adults with job-related or educational objectives and is also available in Spanish. The Kentucky series is designed specifically for adults preparing for the GED examination. The latter series is being used in most areas of the country and in a special project in federal correctional institutions in 33 sites.

A basic education and communication course that is also widely used is "Getting the Word," a series of 30 half-hour lessons devoted to improving communication skills through the use of phonics, linguistics, and language-experience approaches. This series is produced by South Carolina ETV.

Two English as a second language courses are "Time for English" and "Speak for Yourself," distributed respectively by Great Plains national ITV Library and Time-Life. Both consist of 30 half-hour lessons. The former program is adult-directed and the latter is a series of lessons for elementary to advanced learners. "Speak for Yourself" includes an accompanying workbook.

---

[13]Cassettes shown to the staff of the Youth Department, Henry Street Settlement House/Urban Life Center, New York City.

A number of interesting courses have been developed for consumer education. One, familiar to New York viewers of WNET/Channel 13, is "Consumer Survival Kit." This consists of 27 half-hour programs with accompanying materials for each program, including a program summary, pertinent articles, and editorials. Chicago TV College offers a similar program, "Consumer Economics—Dollar Power."

While many other programs are in use in specific regions of the country, these are probably the most widely distributed. We found no record of anything approaching the coordinated British system using open broadcast accompanied by broad community-support systems. When programs like those mentioned above are presented on open broadcast, students are able to purchase workbooks, but there is no related tutorial or class system. Many of the sources are not intended chiefly for open broadcast but are meant for use within ongoing classes or courses managed by state boards of education or with ABE.

Most studies, most notably that done by the Appalachian Adult Education Center (*A Handbook for ETV Utilization in Adult Education*, 1975), stress the importance of linking open-broadcast presentations to a network of counselors, advisers, or teachers who can assist in analyzing individual learning needs and provide encouragement along the way. Such a combination, they suggested, would be the chief element in making mass education via television available to large numbers of learners. This is the approach that has been used effectively with radio in developing countries.

The differences between models 2 and 3 (using broadcast material as a tool for needs assessment and discussion, and using it for presenting subject matter) lie in the educational approach rather than in any specific rationale about television as an educational medium—at least as these models are currently utilized. Both rely at the present time on the distribution of cassettes for use in learning centers, schools, and other settings rather than on open broadcast. They are classroom tools and their use does not advance very much the understanding of broadcasting's potential for reaching wider audiences in the United States.

Other examples exist of reasonably successful pilot efforts to use broadcast technologies in adult education. These include the satellite-broadcast experiments in Appalachia, the Northwest, and Alaska (early 1970s); the satellite experiment in India (early 1970s); the Farm Forum in India (early 1960s); the Telescuola in Italy (1960s); the Radio Sutatenza scheme in Colombia; and others.

The significant conclusion from these is that the technology for delivering visual and auditory material over vast geographic areas is much more highly developed than our capability to organize, fund, and staff the effective educational programs necessary to make full use of the potential of the technology. To date, the more-or-less successful broadcast-based approaches have used the medium to supplement innovative discussion-group and problem-based community activities and programs. Our judgment is that the activities would probably have been about as successful even if the broadcast capability had not been available, although their outreach might not have been as wide.

Conclusion: Broadcast Media—Radio and Television

Is any combination of broadcast media and support services appropriate for use in the United States as a means of involving presently unreached educationally disadvantaged adults? We know already that closed-circuit TV, cassettes, and other broadcast material are being used to advantage in many places. However, no coordination of agencies and resources approaching the British model has been attempted in the United States. A series of problems remains to be solved:

1. The audience that needs to be reached does not at present watch public TV broadcasts.
2. There is a lack of coordination between adult education, technology, and the Commission on Public Broadcasting/Public Broadcasting System. No catalytic leadership has emerged to bridge this gap despite good proposals for the use of open broadcast.
3. A gap exists between the delivery capability of the media and community/regional planning for utilization.

PARTICIPATION AND FUNDING PROBLEMS OF ADULT EDUCATION

Much has been written about the "adult education boom" in this country. Some 32 million adults are said to be enrolled each year. Adults have responded to course offerings for everything from "Slimnastics" to computer-programming and the neuro-sciences. Statistics on participation and costs in adult education are as difficult to assemble as those related to the portion of the population that is educationally disadvantaged. We wish to highlight a few basic facts, however, because they bear on our study.

Participation in adult education activities by adults with low prior levels of education is disproportionately small in comparison with their numbers in the total population. Despite the so-called boom, we know that only between 10 and 20 percent of all adults participate in any planned group-learning activities (Broschart, 1976, p. 28). Of those who do, the smallest percentages are from the segment of the population with the least formal-educational background. Adult education programs in this country primarily serve those who already enjoy most of society's advantages. We have already seen the correlation between low income and low levels of education. Figure 16 shows clearly that those who have less income also enter fewer adult educational activities.

This situation is confirmed in a May 1977 study showing that, while those with less than a high school education make up about 40 percent of the total eligible adult population, they constitute only 13 percent of those participating in adult education (Froomkin and Wolfson, pp. 43–44). Researchers, observing statistical changes in participation in adult education, say that the white and the wealthy have benefited most from increased opportunities for adult education. Between 1969 and 1975, participation by whites increased nearly three times as fast as their population increased, while participation by blacks, in proportion to their numbers, decreased. In 1975, the increased participation by blacks was less than one-third their population increase in the intervening period (Rosenthal, 1976, p. 140).

Reports of the Office of Education and the National Advisory Council on Adult Education indicate that the national average of ABE participants is somewhere between 2 and 4 percent of the total eligible population.[14] As might be expected, minorities are overrepresented among ABE participants. In 1971, only one out of every two students was white; one out of three was black (three times the national proportion); Native Americans, only 0.3 percent of the national population, were registered in ABE at almost four times that ratio; Asians were enrolled at seven times the national figure (NACAE, 1974, p. 68).

The cost of educational services for adults rises in proportion to the degree of disadvantage of those served. Nowhere do statistics exist that might tell us how much adults spend on their own education. Most educators and legislators assume that adults

---

[14]For specific data on federal support for adult basic education, as well as state and local support, and for data on participation by adults in ABE, see the *Report for 1977* of the National Advisory Commission on Adult Education (NACAE), which provides a state-by-state analysis.

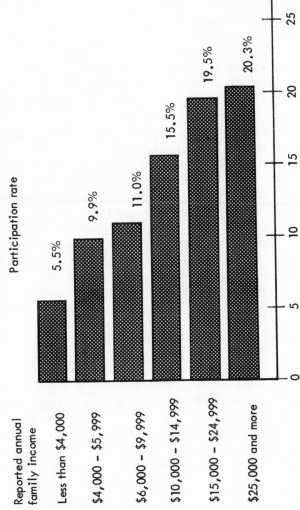

FIGURE 15

Participation in Adult Education by Family Income

(The Condition of Education, 1976, p. 105.)

should pay for their own education. Yet, increasingly, employers subsidize the continuing education of their personnel, adding substantially to the options that already exist for the better educated among the population. In the 1960s, as we noted, social legislation brought into being such programs as ABE and a large number of manpower-training and poverty-related programs. Federal, state, and local contributions to ABE amounted, in 1976, to approximately $260 million (NACAE, 1977b). We do not know the cost of the other programs.

Privately funded adult education "manages itself" according to the model of the marketplace. Public-policy issues about appropriate goals, access to activities, content and methods, the distribution of available resources, and other matters of control arise only in relation to those funded directly out of tax monies (Broschart, 1976, p. 49).

Growing attention to the concept of lifelong learning and the increasing scarcity of financial resources lead some to ask whether sufficient attention has been given to the provision of resources for those most in need of additional education within the society. The *quantity* of money spent on those who are able to do least for themselves will be proportionately greater if the *quality* of services is to be made equally available to all sectors of the adult population. Counseling, transportation, childcare, one-to-one recruitment, in-home service, nonprint information, and electronic-media delivery of services are essential adjuncts to programs for the disadvantaged. The costs of high-quality programs will inevitably be higher for these "stationary poor" than for those who believe in themselves and in the services available to them and who can help to shoulder both responsibility and cost.

Widespread assumptions about access to educational services do not generally take into account the factor of greater need. Many responses to the data showing the low levels of participation in adult education by the educationally disadvantaged attempt to justify that situation. In the hearings on the lifelong-learning legislation, one speaker suggested that the time had come for the government to fund more activities for "regular" adults, since so much was already being spent on "special people" (that is, the disadvantaged). Froomkin and Wolfson's analysis—or reanalysis—of the survey of adult education that was conducted by the National Center of Educational Statistics in 1972 also attempts to justify this situation. "The delivery of adult education," they maintain, "is not as skewed to the rich as is commonly believed.'' They acknowledge that the poor (and the undereducated) do not enroll in adult education programs in proportion to their numbers in the population, but point out that they ''are likely to enroll in courses of longer duration,'' so that ''the demand for *hours* of adult education is distributed in proportion to eligibles in each age and education group'' (Froomkin and Wolfson, 1977, pp. 6–7). This curious rationalization, which underlies the entire study, suggests that each group in the society (the old and the young, the poor and the rich, the undereducated and the well educated) should receive its proportionate ''resource share of adult education.'' In becoming apologists for the statistics, Froomkin and Wolfson lose sight of another goal, which is not the number of adult education course hours consumed, but, rather, meeting the needs of adult learners, particularly those who have been by-passed or outcast by the institutions of society.

Another major study of the cost-benefit relationships growing out of the channeling of federal ABE funds through the public schools, the community colleges, or a combination of the two as these affect the local community, the state, and the nation concludes that no one institution has resources to serve the entire target population (Griffith, 1974). This study makes a case for interinstitutional delivery systems based on carefully worked-out local agreements among both private and public institutions. The study points out that the range of adult education needs is so vast that multiple, carefully planned responses in discrete programs are required. It further recommends that the focus of ABE be integrated into a community-oriented approach.

These three basic facts—that the most-impoverished and least-educated adults participate the least in traditional adult education programs, that the cost of adult education services is higher for the more disadvantaged, and that the greater need of the disadvantaged is ignored in many current assumptions about educational services—provide direct entree into our final chapter. We have defined the problem of adult illiteracy in the United States, we have discussed its extent and characteristics, and we have examined current programs and policies directed at coping with it. Drawing on all of this analysis and description, we turn now to what is perhaps the most difficult task of all: trying to decide what should be done, by whom, how, and in whose interests.

CHAPTER
IV

∽

What Should Be Done, By Whom, And How?

Let us sum up our argument thus far. Adult illiteracy in the United States is a current focus of public attention. Clear and agreed-upon concepts and definitions of literacy—what it is and how it can be measured—do not exist. As a result, even the limited statistics and other data available about the problem fall far short of what is needed and are often confusing if not downright contradictory. Such *caveats* aside, however, it is clear that many millions among the 54 to 64 million American adults who are 16 years of age or older, out of school, and without a high school diploma suffer significant disadvantages because of their limited education. Indeed, studies of functional competency suggest that one in five American adults has difficulty with *many* tasks required in daily living and that more than one-third have trouble with *some* of those tasks.

Since the mid-1960s educators and legislators have seen these 54 to 64 million Americans as the target population for publicly funded programs offering instruction through the secondary school level. Yet only 2 to 4 percent of them ever enter the programs. Obviously many persons within the target group in fact function competently and realize their personal objectives in their own ways, *sans* the benefits of adult education or much formal schooling of any other kind. Nonetheless, an enormous gap remains between the number who seek help and whose who need it. This gap has important implications both for policies and for programs.

In this chapter we present our proposals for new educational initiatives to serve those adults unreached by present programs. The chapter has five sections and within each will be found our conclusions and the recommendations that flow from them. The five sections of the chapter are:

• *Principal Conclusion and Recommendations*. Wherein we state our principal conclusion and our related principal overall recommendation about adult illiteracy in the United States and also present related specific recommendations 1 and 2.

• *Adult Illiteracy Revisited and Recommendations*. Wherein we place changing concepts of literacy and the goal of universal literacy in the dynamic context of broad national goals and present specific recommendation 3.

• *Adult Illiterates Revisited and Recommendations*. Wherein we review the data presented in Chapter II about the characteristics of the educationally disadvantaged in our society, identify four different subgroups of the disadvantaged with different needs, argue that multiple strategies are required to take into account these diverse needs and experiences, and present specific recommendations 4 and 5.

• *Programs and Services Revisited and Recommendations*. Wherein we examine some of the central assumptions of the programs described in Chapter III, conclude that a radically different strategy is necessary to reach the most disadvantaged subgroups, and present specific recommendations 6, 7, 8, and 9.

• *Illiteracy as an Integral Part of the Social and Cultural System and Recommendations*. Wherein we consider again some long-range future strategies which we believe must parallel short-term strategies addressing the immediate needs of specific groups and present our final specific recommendations 10 and 11.

PRINCIPAL CONCLUSION AND RECOMMENDATIONS

Our *principal conclusion* can be briefly stated.

A major shift in national education policy is needed to serve the educational needs of disadvantaged adults.

Our *principal overall recommendation* flowing from that conclusion can also be briefly set forth.

We recommend the establishment of new, pluralistic, com-

munity-based initiatives whose specific objective will be to serve the most *disadvantaged hard-core poor, the bulk of whom never enroll in any existing program.*

These community-based initiatives would focus on persons *in* the communities where they live. The initiatives would require the adults themselves to contribute to designing programs based on concrete learning needs growing out of specific issues affecting their lives in their communities. In addition, the programs that develop from these initiatives would reflect those needs arising from the interaction of their communities with the institutions of the dominant culture. Programs would be action-oriented. They would involve learning by doing and would occur at times and places determined by the community.

We recommend pluralistic approaches because communities and subgroups within the United States differ in their racial, ethnic, cultural, and socioeconomic identities. They differ, too, in their present levels of knowledge, how they process information, their motivation for learning, their consciousness of community identity, and how they interact with the larger surrounding society. Educational substance and methods to implement our recommendation would grow out of direct contact with local communities and with the needs and desires of the people who live in them.

As we formulated our recommendations, we discovered the necessity of clarifying what our proposal is *not*—as well as what it *is*. Think of the mainstream culture and its institutions as forming the central core of a circle, surrounded by an outer circle of subgroups and communities which, while they are part of our society, are in many ways marginal to its life. Indicators of marginality include the extreme poverty of these communities, their unique patterns of language and communication, their diverse cultural values, and their general lack of power to benefit from or to influence the mainstream institutions.

Some advocates of community-based approaches take as their goal the total self-sufficiency and independence of these subgroups, perhaps even creating separate institutions to serve them. In our view this would lead to further marginalization, and isolation. That is not our intent.

We advocate community-based approaches as the means of beginning a reciprocal process of communication and influence. We believe that existing communities and social groups are legitimate sources of personal and group identity. At the same time, however, we support programs that increase the skills of community members to interact with and change the mainstream culture and its institutions. This would incorporate the positive values of the communities and enable their members to partic- ipate more fully in the social and economic life of the broader society.

The remainder of this chapter is devoted to clarifying the prin- cipal recommendation, presenting its underlying rationale, and drawing some of the policy implications that emerge from it. (Each recommendation is recapitulated in Appendix A.)

SPECIFIC RECOMMENDATION 1:

The principal overall recommendation for community-based approaches to the most educationally disadvantaged adults should be given wide dissemination through the distribution of this study to legislators and policy-makers, government officials, corporations and foundations, adult education professionals and practitioners, and those in other disciplines who are concerned with community development. Our goal is to invite response and, where possible, support for the implementation of both the prin- cipal and the specific recommendations.

SPECIFIC RECOMMENDATION 2:

A series of well-publicized regional conferences should be held to gather data and to create a climate for implementing the central proposal for new community-based approaches.

The conferences would include a large group of "clients," representing the young unemployed, older persons, racial and ethnic minorities, aliens, prisoners, and others from specific com- munities and subgroups of the most educationally disadvantaged who are not in any existing programs. These persons would be the *speakers* at the conference. The *hearers* or *learners* would be persons professionally engaged in community services—ed- ucators, social workers, health service personnel, community- development leaders, public administrators—as well as persons from the business community, legislators, representatives of gov- ernment and private-sector funding agencies, and labor leaders. Representatives of the media would be invited and encouraged to give the conferences maximum coverage.

The central purpose of each conference would be to hear from community persons which programs, in their opinion, are working and which are not—and why. No effort would be made to reach definitive conclusions. Rather, the goal would be to gather information that public and private agencies might use to implement the other recommendations of our study and the new recommendations that will emerge as the process develops.

The initiative for organizing the conferences could be taken by either a public or a private agency or by a coalition of interested groups. A government agency or a foundation could start the process by forming an ad hoc coalition. If our hypotheses are valid, the movement will begin to gather its own momentum. Careful preparation would be necessary to build trust in and to give legitimacy to the conferences. Perhaps, guided by the speakers, conferees might go into nearby communities to talk with others from the community as part of the learning process. Or, adopting a tool designed to foster open communication between mine workers and managers in Appalachia, videotaped conversations could be used.

ADULT ILLITERACY REVISITED AND RECOMMENDATIONS

Chapter II identified two factors that make the concept of literacy elusive. First, as a society becomes more complex in both its technology and social institutions, expectations about the skills needed for participation in the society are also raised. Second, concepts of literacy have been extended during recent decades to include far more than conventional reading and writing. Emphasis has been placed on the *uses* of literacy that enable persons to function competently in their daily lives.

We conclude that concepts of literacy will likely always be dynamic and differ both among societies and among diverse subgroups within a given society. We also conclude that individuals are influenced in their opportunities to acquire literacy skills and, therefore, in the importance they assign to literacy by the values of the primary social groups to which they belong. Racial or ethnic discrimination and extreme poverty create barriers inhibiting the full participation of certain groups in the visible rewards of the society and bar these groups from the institutions that serve the dominant social groups. As a result, the expectations about the usefulness of literacy skills are likely to be lower within the excluded groups.

The ability to read and write and to use mathematical symbols is so much a part of the lives of literate persons that they find it almost impossible to imagine themselves without those skills. Literacy skills open the way to information, to the enjoyment of literature, and to certain kinds of communication and self-expression. In a literate society, they also confer independence in managing one's own affairs. They qualify persons for certain credentials. As we noted earlier, however, these formal credentials themselves may weigh more heavily in the competition for jobs than they do as a part of the actual skills required to perform the jobs.

Literate persons often believe that it is their literacy per se that has been responsible for opening doors for them in the society, conferring social status or economic success, or creating their attitudes. They are inclined, therefore, to endorse literacy campaigns under the illusion that illiteracy is the cause of the poverty, ill-health, and the crime-infested neighborhoods in which they see others living.

The solution to the serious problems that afflict the majority of illiterates is not so simple. Their problems are inextricably interwoven with class, race, and their access to power. By the time they are adults, those who are caught in a complex of social and economic disadvantages suffer multiple impediments that cannot be removed by learning to read or write. The value of literacy is enhanced for them only when it can be useful in the course of achieving their goals in a wide range of life-influencing areas: economic security, health care, greater power over decisions affecting their families, better schools for their children, community improvement, and the like. The process of meeting their more pressing social and economic needs will also broaden the context within which they can use literacy skills.

Similarly, mass literacy does not cure the corporate ills of a society: unemployment, poverty, discrimination, or the marginal status of certain subgroups. However, when the society itself assumes the responsibility to combat these conditions as a central goal, and when visible progress is being made in reforming economic and social institutions, the number on persons and groups that achieve higher standards of literacy will likely increase.

An Israeli educator noted that it is in times of ferment and dramatic social change that adult education flourishes (Grebelsky & Yaron, 1972). The rapid increases in the literacy rates of China, Cuba, Tanzania, Israel and, to some degree, Brazil, confirm this. Literacy is an accompaniment to rather than a prime cause of social progress. In industrialized nations like our own, groups that have already been successfully incorporated into the economic and social system seek and achieve higher levels of literacy. Conversely, marginal groups have the highest proportions of illiterates.

Reading and writing at relatively high levels of competence are important within the United States today. They are tools that can be used, however, only by those who are in all other respects full members of the society, able to achieve their basic human objectives within it.

A society's concepts of literacy are a function both of its technological, social, and economic development and of its goals and expectations about the quality of life for all citizens. We must dispel two myths: that literacy is the primary *cause* of progress; and that illiteracy is the cause of poverty and injustice. Only then can we place responsibility for change where it belongs, at the center of social and economic planning; only then can we make more realistic appraisals of the values of literacy as these inform the expectations of both literate and illiterate adults.

SPECIFIC RECOMMENDATION 3:

The persons who take part in the regional conferences (Recommendation 2) should develop appropriate means within their own geographic areas to:

increase public awareness of the needs of marginal communities in their locales;

involve other educators and service professionals in direct contacts with community people around the same concerns addressed in the original conferences;

encourage the preparation of concept papers on the social context of literacy based on this experience; and

begin to compile an inventory of successful community-based programs already going on in their area.

ADULT ILLITERATES REVISITED AND RECOMMENDATIONS

Chapter II noted that the available statistics reveal only the rough outlines of the population groups within which are found those with the most serious literacy problems. The problems are most acute for those who have not completed elementary school. Those adults 16 years and older not enrolled in school and without high school diplomas numbered between 54 and 64 million persons. The Adult Performance Level (APL) study of functional competence confirmed that this group included both those persons severely and those partially handicapped in performing tasks commonly required of adults in this society.

Those who have not completed high school earn less than those who have. They are more likely to be unemployed or on welfare. They are found in disproportionate numbers in the South and the East. Many are in rural areas, but the majority are in urban centers—generally in the decaying inner-cities. The number from minority groups—blacks, persons of Hispanic origin, Native Americans—is disproportionately high, although the gap is narrowing. Potentially, the most serious situation is that of the young who are presently dropping out of school, among whom unemployment rates are highest, who will soon become parents themselves, and who will comprise a substantial proportion of future adult illiterates.

What do we really know when we have examined all these facts? Those who gather statistics about a specific issue are often tempted to speak as though those affected by it were all alike. Anecdotal data, interviews, the experiences of persons working in tutoring and basic education programs for adults, and some preliminary ethnographic and case-history studies suggest that adult illiterates are at least as varied and disparate as any other statistically defined agglomeration.

An inherent risk lies in attempting to establish categories when talking about human beings. Yet the opposite risk, blurring the genuine distinctions in the situations, needs, and aspirations of those with educational deficiencies, may be even more serious when an attempt to develop multiple strategies is being made. A balanced approach to research is needed to obtain accurate and systematic data that does not distort reality and that is useful for policy-making.

We referred in Chapter II to the four broad categories of educationally disadvantaged adults described by the Appalachian Adult Education Center. Our way of seeing the same diversity is to envision a broad spectrum with overlapping and shifting groups and persons. As we sorted through the descriptive data, we were able to identify four focal points on the spectrum of adult illiteracy that may help us to realize the need for a number of quite different educational strategies.

Group I. At one end, let us say the far right, are those who share most fully the values of the dominant cultural group within the

U.S. These persons may have dropped out of school for personal reasons—the need to help with family support, an early marriage, a school unable to engage their interest—yet they continue to learn. Many engage in nonformal learning activities, take occasional courses in pursuit of their personal interests, or simply read what is available. Most are regularly employed or keep house and raise families. The persons around them in their families and communities are upwardly mobile and have probably completed high school. The major stumbling block for such persons is their lack of those credentials that the society values so highly. They are embarrassed by not having a high school diploma and find this the most significant barrier to self-esteem and job advancement. These are the persons who succeed in passing high school equivalency exams when they make serious attempts to study the required materials. The traditional classroom patterns do not entirely put them off, although they respond more readily to programs that give them credit for the learning they have done over the years. Case studies of those who enrolled in the various external high school diploma programs have provided a good picture of these adults. A number of them go on to further studies when they have acquired the high school credentials.

Also within this group are persons who have recently come to the United States from other parts of the world. Their education in their own countries may be roughly comparable to that of those persons described above, yet their language difficulties, compounded by the lack of an American high school diploma, force them to take lower-paying jobs. When they do enter language classes, they do well. They, too, respond readily to opportunities to learn and expect to fit into a classroom approach. (We do not include the professionals who come from abroad with advanced degrees and who require only language training. They are not among the educationally disadvantaged.)

Group 2. At a second, quite different point on the spectrum, just to the left of the first group, are persons with far more serious educational deficiencies. They leave school earlier than the first group. Some never learned to read and write at all. Yet they belong to social groups in which literacy is taken for granted. Some have married literate persons. Some have jobs that require more literacy skills than they possess. For them it is not merely the lack of a diploma that causes them embarrassment but, rather, the tasks they simply are not able to perform. Many live in constant fear of being "found out." They go to extreme pains to hide their problem, constantly being "caught without their glasses" or having "headaches" just when they see that they may be required to read something in a group. The stigma of being illiterate accompanies them constantly. Coming out and admitting their problems is highly emotional and difficult. A precipitating experience of acute discomfort may send some for help. They often go to another town to study or find some other environment where they are not known. Many of these persons can be reached through intensive campaigns like the BBC program in Great Britain or the Laubach (NALA) or Literary Volunteers of America (LVA) recruitment efforts. They are the ones about whom the "success" stories are often written. Their literacy problems may cause them more distress than that felt by many far to the left on the spectrum precisely because, as nonreaders among literate peers, they are exceptions within their own social communities and sometimes even within their own families. Overcoming their difficulties causes such dramatic changes in their personal lives that they speak of the change almost as though it were a religious conversion.

Group 3. Further to the left are persons who suffer multiple deprivations. They live in the inner-city or in rural poverty areas. The lack of credentials and the inability to perform tasks associated with literacy are only a small part of their lives. The majority of this group left school because they were failing. They could see little immediate pay-off in continuing schooling. As adults they sometimes try again by entering ABE or similar programs. Too often, their earlier, unsuccessful experience is repeated. Those who persevere nourish a dim hope that self-sacrifice and greater efforts on their part will, finally, make a difference. Job-training programs have considerable appeal to them as alternatives to traditional schooling.

Also within this group are many whose first language is either a nonstandard form of English or some other language. These persons have had little formal education. Whether they are native-born Americans, legal aliens, recently naturalized persons, or undocumented aliens, they are generally employed in menial jobs or find work only intermittently.

Group 4. The group just described—both English and non-English speaking—merges on the spectrum with another group, similar to them yet different in one important aspect: the level of hope that can be kindled in them—even temporarily. Persons in this fourth group have largely given up believing that anything they can do will make a difference in their overall situations. They are the hard-core stationary poor, the persons described by Michael Harrington and other writers as the "forgotten" or "invisible" poor. They may live in the very shadow of major institutions of health-care or education yet receive no benefits from those institutions. Their interaction with the majority culture is minimal. Encounters with bureaucracies set up to serve them—employment, housing, health services, their children's schools, the welfare system, the courts—all contribute to their sense of defeat and help perpetuate the cycles of deprivation and alienation. While some of them may continue to believe that things can be better for their children, the model they present— all too visible to their offspring—of powerlessness and marginality, often leads their children to pursue money and power through illegal means or to sink into the parental despair.

Our data—soft, partially unreliable, impressionistic though they may be—lead us to recommend new approaches to the groups near the third and fourth points on the spectrum, groups that may include 18 to 28 million adult Americans. Parallel with new program initiatives addressed to persons in communities, we also need to learn more about the human beings on this end of the spectrum and their needs as they see them, as well as the strengths within their communities that enable them to survive. We will make recommendations about the programmatic implications of our conclusion at the end of the next section on programs and services.

The descriptions above stress the negative aspects of the hard-core poor's existence, but it is also significant that the demands of their circumstances and the persistence of adaptive cultural traits have enabled communities of the poor to develop qualities of family and group solidarity often absent in the dominant, individualistic society. These Americans live in circumstances that most of us would find intolerable, yet strong patterns of interaction, mutual support, information exchange, and personal loyalty are also present in their lives. We and they need to understand better the realities of these communities and subgroups if any effective action is to emerge that will change what is, by simultaneously building on strengths and combating oppressive forces.

SPECIFIC RECOMMENDATION 4:

A more systematic and accurate data base about the groups, communities, and general population with which we are concerned should be developed and widely disseminated in diverse forms appropriate to the multiplicity of potential users.

This recommendation might be carried out by a cross-disciplinary coalition of university personnel and private agencies. The coalition would survey existing research and anthropological and ethnographic studies of rural and urban American communities. Attempts would be made to discover whether answers already exist to the following questions and to others that may occur in the process of conceptualizing the new approaches to communities and groups within them:

• What are the characteristics and learning needs of the most educationally disadvantaged community groups?
• What factors are essential to understanding a particular community?
• Can data-gathering instruments be developed that will enable community members to participate in discovering their own community profile?
• What factors contribute to building trust between outside groups and community persons so that both studies and programs can be carried on "with" and not "for" them?
• Are there internal or external factors that contribute to community cohesiveness?
• What criteria can be used to determine the effectiveness of organizations and programs within the life of a community?

SPECIFIC RECOMMENDATION 5:

A consultation should be arranged to bring together those most active in relevant research efforts to exchange information and plan together for other needed research.

This step would, of necessity, follow recommendation 4 and would be taken only if it appeared that a greater coordination of efforts would stimulate and clarify research. We believe that more is going on in this field than is understood in any one place.

PROGRAMS AND SERVICES REVISITED AND RECOMMENDATIONS

Chapter III examined a wide range of educational programs and services. Some programs concentrated on teaching conven-

tional literacy. Others offered courses leading toward the ful-
fillment of elementary or secondary school equivalency requirements. A growing number of programs are emphasizing the
acquisition of functional skills basic to competency in everyday
adult tasks. Despite the variations in objectives and emphases,
the most frequently mentioned problem area was the same for
all programs: the recruitment and retention of learners.

Preoccupation with attendance and with getting students into
the programs and keeping them once they are enrolled stems
from the continuing emphasis placed on the size of the gap between the so-called target population (54 to 64 million) and the
demand population (the 2 to 4 million who actually enroll). We
believe that the pressure on program administrators to reach the
whole population of educationally disadvantaged adults is the
result of a failure to make sufficiently clear distinctions among
the quite different needs of those within the target group.

Those responsible for educational programs spend considerable time and energy attempting to convince adults that the specific skills offered by their programs are, in fact, useful; that the
programs actually provide the skills they promise; and that the
skills in question will enable those who possess them to accomplish their personal goals.

We believe that present programs and the results they promise
are, in fact, primarily valid for adults in Group 1, on the far right
of the spectrum described above. Education is highly valued in
their primary social groups. They are able to see evidence in the
lives of those around them that their situations have been improved by obtaining credentials and skills. Since the personal
motivation and self-confidence of these adults are strong, they
are able to buy into the hope that through their personal efforts
they can move up on the social and economic ladder or, at the
very least, feel better about themselves and increase their stature
in the eyes of their families and associates.

Those responsible for ABE and similar programs should concentrate on this specific constituency that finds more traditional
patterns of schooling congenial.[1] With this clearer focus, these
programs might implement some of the reforms already rec-

---

[1]One study, in 1967, concluded that ABE would have to undergo radical changes
if it were to serve the real needs of the illiterate poor. It would have to move
away from a traditional school model and towards a social-action model, which
would emphasize social and civic problems of the poor as well as educational
problems (*Federally Funded Adult Basic Education Programs*, 1967).

ommended by studies of their operation and thus be better able to serve their clients. We believe that the most critical areas of change include:

- defining more specifically the constituency that can be reached by "second chance" opportunities offered through traditional educational structures and models;
- establishing local and regional learning centers in which all the resources of the community are known and where individuals can be guided to programs that best suit their needs;
- establishing closer relationships between tutoring programs and those that provide classwork in both conventional and functional skill areas so that students may more readily move from one to the other;
- sponsoring carefully planned campaigns in the media that legitimize the pursuit of skills by adults of any age; and
- clarifying the objectives of programs so that they do not promise more than they can deliver but still emphasize the value of increased educational attainment.

We also see the continuation of studies and program development growing out of APL (Adult Performance Level) as valuable for improving traditional programs, developing new programs that focus on competence and coping skills, and establishing a knowledge base about requirements for successful participation in adult life in a complex technological environment. (The temptation to freeze approaches and to make broad generalizations should be resisted, however. Present testing instruments may have only limited usefulness unless considerably more attention is given to differences among subgroups within the target population.)

APL-related curriculum materials and some of the television cassettes for public broadcast and small-group use are effective for adults on the right-hand half of the spectrum because they are based on middle-class assumptions about options available to individuals within the society.

The use of videotape and audio-visual materials in community-based settings requires considerably more study of the factors that condition the lives of the most disadvantaged.

The voluntary tutoring programs also reach a distinct, identifiable constituency. From 30 to 40 thousand adults whose primary social groups are made up of literate persons seek tutoring annually. Many of these Group 2 persons are starting from absolute zero in literacy skills. We believe that many more would come forward for help if the stigma of illiteracy were lessened through public efforts to demonstrate that it is not unique and that others have overcome illiteracy and thereby improved their lives. The task should not be left to the limited resources of private agencies alone. Their experience, however, should be appropriated and far more extensive efforts made to build on the models and methods they have developed. (To extend the model to *different* constituencies requires new approaches that we will describe below.)

In sum, we suggest that persons and groups on the right-hand half of the spectrum described above are appropriate present or potential clients of existing programs. The key to effective participation in schooling programs, tutoring, and functional-skills training seems to be the degree of confidence possessed by individuals (and by the social groups and communities to which they belong) that they are personally responsible for their successes and failures. The fact that they do make progress in the programs strengthens their resolve. Unfortunately, this concept is shared by almost everyone, and that is why the poor have such a personally low self-image in addition to feeling powerless (that is, many feel that, if they were smarter, they would have "made it" somehow).

For persons on the left-hand end of the spectrum (Groups 3 and 4), the situation is quite different. Their experience has been filled with failures to "make it" in society. Those in their primary social groups who have succeeded have moved on to other communities, other jobs, other lives. Those who remain are oppressed by multiple problems over which they appear to have little control. Either no solutions are apparent or they appear to lie somewhere else. Persons in Groups 3 and 4 are inhibited by so many other insurmountable difficulties that both their motivation and energy are very low or entirely absent.

We believe that great efforts are already being expended on meeting the needs of those who can be well served by existing programs. Therefore, our specific recommendations focus almost entirely on the most disadvantaged, hardest to reach adults. As we stated at the beginning of this chapter, we believe that a major new initiative is necessary—one that provides genuine alternatives to schooling by establishing pluralistic community-based programs.

Among the programs that we examined in the study, a few were community-based and included learning in the context of specific community objectives that had significance for the individuals and families involved—the Southern Christian Leadership Conference voter-education project, the Native American survival schools, and the San Antonio Barrio Education Project. These programs are isolated examples of the approach we recommend on a far broader scale. Much can be learned by an analysis of the origins, successes, and failures of these and similar programs.

We would like to see not only a multiplication of similar efforts but a national policy funded to promote this approach to adults and to the communities in which they live. The people themselves would have the major voice in the determination of what they and their communities want to work on—whether securing better health services, cleaning up the neighborhood, improving the schools, learning how to deal with the bureaucracies in their lives, developing small businesses, gaining skills needed to secure employment, organizing to achieve political goals, or replacing entrenched "bosses" or interests working against the welfare of the community.

Starting from such immediate and practical concerns, the "curriculum" of action and learning from that action would be developed. The generative themes of the community (the most significant concerns of community life) would emerge and necessary learning tasks could be identified. Learning and meeting sites should be "on the block," that is, in places already recognized as belonging to the community. These might be churches, homes, or community centers—wherever people feel comfortable when they congregate.

Leadership would have to be chosen by the community and trained in nonformal educational methods. Persons from outside the immediate communities might fulfill some of these roles, but opportunities must be made for testing the validity of homegrown and outside leadership within the community. Groups and classes should be so formed as to enable people to work and learn with their friends, families, and neighbors, not apart from them as the present programs require. Methods would conform to the needs of the groups involved; learning resources would be gathered or developed by and for the specific requirements of the persons involved.

Tutors specifically prepared to do individual tutoring should be available to those who need this service. We believe that present voluntary tutoring programs could help to prepare persons from the community to serve as individual tutors.

It is abundantly clear that the resources of a wide range of professional disciplines and organizations would have to be part of organizing such a program. It is equally clear that intensive efforts would be required to enable these "outsiders" to understand the concerns of the communities. The often-described and seldom-practiced requirement of learning *with* persons of different social and cultural experiences is the essential ingredient for meaningful participation of educators, social workers, public service personnel, health workers, community development specialists, and other experts in the program we are recommending.

SPECIFIC RECOMMENDATION 6:

As answers to the questions under recommendation 4 become available, and as regional groups begin to develop information about communities where successful programs are underway, several case studies should be undertaken to provide information about:
- past and present experience in the successful integration of community development and adult education goals;
- different models of financing these programs and information about levels of funding necessary for minimum and maximum accomplishment for a variety of programs;
- alternative approaches that provide flexibility for indigenous groups to accomplish their own goals;
- a variety of mechanisms for integrated local planning and management of projects that cut across traditional lines of functional responsibility—community development, health services, education, job training, and the like;
- a list of competencies that community members believe are necessary for the full participation of their members to assume greater responsibility for community life; and
- strategies for maintaining programs free of political control by self-selected "managers" from inside or outside the community.

SPECIFIC RECOMMENDATION 7:

Educational agencies and organizations should be encouraged and enabled by appropriate funding to establish a number of pilot projects to test the hypotheses of this study and others emanating from work carrying out the earlier recommendations.

This recommendation might be implemented by adding a research and evaluation dimension to already existing programs or by establishing new projects. We suggest the following criteria for the selection of projects.

• There should be opportunity to test interdisciplinary training for teacher/enablers to work in the project. (This training would draw on the resources of schools of education, social work, community development, public administration, health services, etc., and would develop skills in the assessment of community needs, the discovery of generative themes in the life of the community, the use of local resources and methods for developing student-generated materials, strategies for relating community needs and individual learning needs, and program evaluation based on the accomplishment of community and learner objectives.)

• The program should be staffed by persons from the community or acceptable to the community—i.e., chosen according to criteria they determine.

• There should be maximum opportunity for client participation in the planning and implementation of the project.

• The program should provide a genuine alternative to the traditional schooling.

• Wherever possible, the language of the family and immediate social group of those for whom the program is planned should be used.[2]

SPECIFIC RECOMMENDATION 8:

A national commission on community-based initiatives should be established to provide visibility for the recommended new approaches and to provide leadership in the accomplishment of those tasks that *must* be done nationally. These tasks might include:

• the formulation and recommendation of policy proposals necessary to institutionalize community-based approaches;

• the writing of recommendations for legislation to implement the policies;

• the drafting of proposals to secure public funding;

---

[2]The use of the primary language is particularly significant at the beginning of the program. One of the early needs identified by the community may well be to learn to function in the "dominant" standard English. Efforts must be made and care taken, however, not to denigrate the communication patterns already in common use within the community, whether those be variants of standard English or another language.

• the education of the public about the significance of the new approaches to communities; and

• communication of experimental and research findings to professionals and practitioners.

The recommendation for a national commission has been delayed until now because, while national coordination and visibility are important components of any new strategy, the essential element in our proposal is the emphasis on *pluralistic local initiatives*. Independent responses to, and ad hoc coalitions formed to address, different aspects of the proposal appear to provide a starting point that is both more consistent with the spirit of the proposal itself and more promising in terms of assuring that interested persons and agencies will be able to bring their own enthusiasms to launching the idea. When, how, or if a national commission comes into being will depend on factors that we cannot foresee before there has been both considerable local action and evidence of interest among national agencies.

SPECIFIC RECOMMENDATION 9:

Background studies should be undertaken and alternative proposals tested to determine the most effective ways to obtain legislation and funding necessary if the new approaches are to be implemented nationally on a scale commensurate with the need.

A national commission, if such comes into being, would be the appropriate body to implement this recommendation. If not, a small group familiar with government requirements and procedures—and including HEW personnel interested in the proposals—might be formed to accomplish this task. Some of the questions requiring answers are:

• How can legislation be enacted that would make funds from a variety of governmental sources directly available to community groups, by-passing entrenched bureaucracies and at the same time guaranteeing necessary reporting and accountability?

• What legislation would be necessary to secure funding from educational sources for programs that do not "look like" education?

• What legislation would be necessary at the state level to enable such structures as existing community learning centers to become centers for information and resource distribution in a wider range of areas, including health, education,

welfare, employment—able to meet the needs without un-
necessary delays and red tape? (Our thought is that such
centers might become the places where action, skill training,
and learning needs could be identified with groups and individuals, and programs designed to meet those needs as
well as information supplied about appropriate community
resources.)

ILLITERACY AS AN INTEGRAL PART OF THE
SOCIAL AND CULTURAL SYSTEM: OVERVIEW AND
RECOMMENDATIONS

Education has the potential for resolving some of the problems
and meeting some of the needs of educationally disadvantaged
adults. An underlying theme that has emerged through this study
is that adult illiteracy cannot be seen or treated in isolation. A
substantial number of adults are seriously disadvantaged not only
with respect to education but to a whole cluster of other significant social benefits: employment, housing, food, health care,
and public services. Each manifestation of disadvantage is related
to the others. The roots of these problems in adult life reach
back into schools that track children for social roles according
to the wealth and status of their parents (Persell, 1977). They
reach into an economic system that does not provide full employment except in time of war (Best and Stern, 1976). They
reach into the cultural processes of child-rearing that institutionalize attitudes of superiority and inferiority along racial, ethnic, sex, age, and class lines (McDermott, 1974).

In earlier times in American history, it was perhaps possible
to believe that each individual determined his or her destiny. At
least since World War II, however, a drastically changed social
environment has developed. This country's frontiers are no
longer geographic or physical; they are now frontiers of purpose
and values. It is precisely because the United States is techno-
logically advanced and economically developed that a challenge
is posed. For the first time, the quality of life for the whole
population is at issue.

Scientific technology enabled us to enter outer space and has
substantially changed life for millions. Yet, unease is growing
over the modern societies' inability to control the consequences
of the growth of knowledge. Scientists know what we *can* do.

They and others are beginning to ask what we *ought* to do. Questions of social need and social interest are receiving attention in many quarters. A recent issue of *Daedalus*, for example, was devoted entirely to articles setting forth the dilemmas caused by the potential impact of new scientific knowledge and technology on social institutions and, indeed, on all life. The issue of the kind of world and the quality of life we want is of such consequence that it cannot be resolved by narrow circles of specialists. Political institutions and mechanisms are needed that allow far wider participation of the public in questions affecting not only American society but the future of the planet ("Limits of the Scientific Inquiry," *Daedalus*, Spring 1978).

We advocate new approaches to the most educationally disadvantaged in the communities where they live. This is our short-range strategy. It addresses an immediate problem.

A long-range strategy should involve not only the victims of social ills, but persons and groups at every level of our common life in a serious confrontation with questions of social direction. What is our development *for*? What degree of sacrifice are we willing to undergo to eliminate the waste of human and physical resources in the world? What are the implications of any particular option for ourselves and for others?

SPECIFIC RECOMMENDATION 10:

Citizen groups should be encouraged and enabled to address questions of social purpose through the provision of concrete, issue-oriented resource materials and agenda items about specific problem areas. At the same time, these resource materials and agenda items should be oriented toward the construction of new options for the future.

Study and action groups exist throughout American society. They grapple with issues of energy, nuclear arms, peace, ecology, foreign policy, world hunger, and international development, to name only a few. Some are locally based and independent. Others are tied to national or international networks. We propose to take advantage of the increasing desire of American citizens to play a more significant part in action and thought directed at improving the human prospect. We do not believe that the model society for the future exists anywhere. Whenever an ideal is approached, it requires new evaluation because all social structures demand constant reformation in the light of new experience.

SPECIFIC RECOMMENDATION 11:

There should be instruments for social planning at the national level comparable to those that exist for economic planning.

There has never been a "Council of Social Advisers to the President" or a "Joint Social Affairs Committee of the Congress" to parallel similar structures for economic planning. National policies are more closely related to and based on fiscal concerns than to social-planning considerations. Proposals for instruments for social planning have been before the Congress for the last decade but have never received sufficient support to assure passage. We urge that the whole subject be reviewed and appropriate legislative action taken.

EPILOGUE

We believe that a strategy for involving citizens of all classes and social groups in consideration of national goals, values, and directions is essential if we are to build a society in which all groups and individuals are able to enjoy the full benefits of the society—including educational advantages.

The focus on persons-in-communities is essential not only for new approaches to the educationally disadvantaged, but also to form a broader base of opinion and action in the nation. Only thus can we understand the root causes of illiteracy and develop national strategies to eliminate it.

We believe that our human and economic resources are equal to the issues we face. We have confidence, therefore, in the potential power of these proposals and look forward eagerly to the dialogue we hope they will provoke.

REFERENCES

The Adult Basic Education Program: Progress in Reducing Illiteracy and Improvements Needed. General Accounting Office. Report to Congress. Washington, D.C.: U.S. Office of Education, 1975.

Adult Education Act, Public Law 91-230, and all of its amendments through October 1976.

Adult Functional Competency: A Report to the Office of Education Dissemination Review Panel. Austin, Texas: Division of Extension, University of Texas, 1975a.

Adult Functional Competency: A Summary. Austin, Texas: Division of Extension, University of Texas, 1975b. ERIC ED 114 609.

APL. See *Adult Functional Competency*.

Appalachian Adult Education Center. *Community Education: Final Report*. Morehead, Ky.: Morehead University, 1975.

Barrio Education Project. *Education, Critical Awareness, Participation*. San Antonio: n.d.

Bazany, M.; Badizadegan, M.; Kaufmann, H. D.; and Khosrowshahi, K. *Registration, Participation and Attendance in Functional Literacy Courses*. Work-Oriented Adult Literacy Pilot Project in Iran. Evaluation Studies No. 2. Esfahan, Iran: 1970a.

Bazany, M.; Kaufmann, H. D.; and Safavi, A. *Demographic Characteristics and Interest in Participation in Functional Literacy Courses*. Work-Oriented Adult Literacy Pilot Project in Iran. Evaluation Studies No. 4. Esfahan, Iran: 1970b.

Bazany, M. *Work-Oriented Adult Literacy in Iran: An Experiment: Analysis, Optimalization and Comparisons of the Method*. Vol. 6, Final Technical Report. Esfahan, Iran: 1973.

Beder, Harold W., III. "Community Linkages in Urban Public School Adult Basic Education Programs: A Study of Co-Sponsorship and the Use of Community Liaison Personnel." Unpublished Ph.D. dissertation. New York: Columbia University, 1972.

Best, Fred, and Stern, Barry. *Lifetime Distribution of Education, Work, and Leisure: Research, Speculations, and Policy Implications*. Washington, D.C.: Institution for Educational Leadership, Postsecondary Education Convening Authority, 1976.

Bibliography of Reading Materials for Basic Reading and English as a Second Language. Syracuse, N.Y.: Literacy Volunteers of America, 1976.

Blaug, M. "Literacy and Economic Development." In *The School Review*, Vol. 74, 1966, pp. 394–418.

Brehmer, Margaret, ed. *AIM: A Creative Approach to Teaching Adults*. New York: World Education, 1977.

Broschart, James R. *A Synthesis of Selected Manuscripts about the Education of Adults in the United States*. Prepared for the Bureau of Occupational and Adult Education. Washington, D.C.: U.S. Office of Education, 1976.

Burch, Sandra. "Instead of Corner Hustlers, Youth Emulate Police Team." In *The News and Courier, Charleston Evening Post, SUNDAY*. Charleston, S.C.: July 10, 1977.

Carroll, John B., and Chall, Jeanne, eds. *Toward a Literate Society*. New York: McGraw-Hill Book Company, 1975.

Centers for Community Education Development. Brochure published by C. S. Mott Foundation. Flint, Mich.: 1975.

Childers, Thomas, assisted by Post, Joyce A. *The Information-Poor in America*. Metuchen, N.J.: The Scarecrow Press, Inc., 1975.

Clark, Septima. *Echo in My Soul*. New York: E. P. Dutton Co., 1962.

Clearinghouse For Community Based Free Standing Educational Institutions, Directory of Members, 1978. Washington, D.C.: The Clearinghouse, 1978.

Collins, Randall. "Some Comparative Principles of Educational Stratification." In *Harvard Educational Review*, Vol. 47, No. 1, February 1977.

Colvin, Ruth. *I Speak English*. A Tutor's Guide to Teaching Conversational English. Syracuse, N.Y.: Literacy Volunteers of America, 1976.

Colvin, Ruth, and Root, Jane H. *Read. Reading Evaluation–Adult Diagnosis*. Syracuse, N.Y.: Literacy Volunteers of America, 1972.

Colvin, Ruth, and Root, Jane H. *Tutor. Techniques Used in the Teaching of Reading*. Syracuse, N.Y.: Literacy Volunteers of America, 1976.

Competency-Based Adult Education Profile and Related Resources. Washington, D.C.: Division of Adult Education, U.S. Office of Education, 1976.

Competency-Based Adult Education Report. Washington, D.C.: Division of Adult Education, U.S. Office of Education, 1976.

The Condition of Education. A Statistical Report on the Condition of American Education together with A Description of the Activities of the National Center for Education Statistics. Washington, D.C.: National Center for Education Statistics, March 1976.

Coombs, Philip H., with Prosser, Roy C., and Ahmed, Manzoor. *New Paths to Learning for Rural Children and Youth*. New York: International Council for Educational Development, 1973.

Current Population Reports. P-20, No. 295. Washington, D.C.: U.S. Bureau of the Census, 1976.

Devereux, W. A. "The Adult Literacy Campaign in the United Kingdom." In *Convergence*, Vol. 10, No. 1, 1977.

The Educational Programs of Laubach Literacy International. Brochure. Syracuse, N.Y.: Laubach Literacy International, 1976.

Evaluation of the Community-Based Right to Read Program. Berkeley, Calif.: Pacific Training and Technical Assistance Program, 1974.

The Experimental World Literacy Program: A Critical Assessment. Compiled by the Secretariats of UNESCO and UNDP. Paris: UNESCO Press, 1976.

Federally Funded Adult Basic Education Programs. New York: Xerox Corporation, 1967.

Fisher, Donald L. *Functional Literacy and the Schools.* Washington, D.C.: National Institute of Education, 1978.

Flores, Gerardo. "The Study of Functional Literacy for Citizenship in the Philippines." In *The Quarterly Bulletin of Fundamental Education*, Vol. 2, No. 3, July 1950.

Freire, Paulo. *Pedagogy of the Oppressed.* New York: Seabury Press, 1970.

Froomkin, Joseph, and Wolfson, Robert. *Adult Education 1972: A Re-Analysis.* Washington, D.C.: Educational Policy and Research Center 1977.

GAO. See *The Adult Basic Education Program.*

Gardner, John W. *Excellence: Can We Be Equal and Excellent, Too?* New York: Harper and Row, 1961.

General Description of Programs and Services. Syracuse, N.Y.: Literacy Volunteers of America, n.d.

Gotsick, Priscilla, et al. *Information for Everyday Survival.* Chicago: American Library Association, 1976.

Grebelsky, Ora, and Yaron, Kalman. "Trends in Adult Education in Israel." In *Lifelong Education in Israel.* Jerusalem: The Public Advisory Council on Adult Education, the Adult Education Association of Israel, the Israel National Commission for UNESCO, 1972.

Greenleigh Associates. *Participants in the Field Test of Four Adult Basic Education Systems.* A Follow-up Study. New York: 1968.

Griffith, William S., and Cervero, Ronald M. *The Adult Performance Level Program: A Serious and Deliberate Examination.* An address presented at a session sponsored by the AEA/NAPCAE Convention, New York, N.Y., Nov. 20, 1976.

Griffith, William S., et al. *Public Policy in Financing Basic Education for Adults.* An Investigation of the Cost-Benefit Relationship in Adult Basic Education in Public Schools and Community Colleges. Vol. 1, Summary and Recommendations. Chicago: Department of Education, University of Chicago, May 1974.

A Guide to Using Language Experience with Adults. Cambridge, Mass.: Community Learning Center, 1973. ERIC ED 103 6000.

A Handbook for ETV Utilization in Adult Education. Vol. 3, Final Report. Morehead, Ky.: Appalachian Adult Education Center, 1975.

Hargreaves, David. *On the Move: The BBC's Contribution to the Adult Literacy Campaign in the United Kingdom Between 1972 and 1976.* London: BBC Education, Summer 1977.

Harman, David. *Community Fundamental Education.* Lexington, Mass.: D. C. Heath & Co., 1974.

Harris, Louis, and Associates. *The 1971 National Reading Difficulty Index.* New York: 1971. ERIC ED 057 312.

Heart of the Earth Survival School. Minneapolis: Longie Printing Co., 1976.

Interrelating Library and Basic Education Services for Disadvantaged Adults: A Demonstration of Four Alternative Working Models. Annual Report, Vol. 2. Morehead, Ky.: Appalachian Adult Education Center, 1973.

Jones, H. A. "Adult Literacy in the United Kingdom." In *Convergence,* Vol. 10, No. 1, 1977.

"Just Around the Corner," *Prospectus.* The APL-ETV Project: A Functional Approach to Adult Education. The Mississippi Authority for Educational Television, October 1975.

"Just Around the Corner," *Teachers' Guide.* The Mississippi Authority for Educational Television, 1976.

"Just Around the Corner," *Student Book,* Series 1. New York: Cambridge Book Co., 1977.

Kansas City School District. *Special Project for Coordinated Adult Basic Education, 1968–69.* Final Report. Kansas City, Mo.: 1969. ERIC ED 061 475.

Korf, Michele J. *Feasibility Study: Fundamental Adult Education Services and the Role of Instructional Television.* Report prepared for Educational Broadcasting Corporation WNET/13. Unpublished. New York: WNET/13, 1976.

Leader's Handbook. Basic Reading Tutor Training Workshop. Syracuse, N.Y.: Literacy Volunteers of America, 1975.

Lerner, David. *The Passing of Traditional Society.* New York: The Free Press, 1958.

Lewis, Oscar. *La Vida.* New York: Random House, 1968.

Liebow, Elliot, *Tally's Corner: A Study of Negro Streetcorner Men.* Boston: Little Brown and Co., 1967.

Lifetime Learning Act, 1975. Hearing Before the Subcommittee on Education of the Committee on Labor and Public Welfare. U.S. Senate, 94th Cong., Dec. 18, 1975.

"Limits of the Scientific Inquiry." In *Daedalus*, Vol. 107, No. 2, Spring 1978.

Literacy as a Factor in Development. Paris: UNESCO, Minedlit/3 1965.

Lusterman, Seymour. "Education for Work." In *The Conference BoardRECORD*, Vol. 13, No. 5, May 1976. New York: The Conference Board.

McDermott, R. P. "Achieving School Failure: An Anthropological Approach to Illiteracy and Social Stratification." In *Education and Cultural Process*, George D. Spindler, ed. New York: Holt, Rinehart and Winston, 1974.

MacDonald, Bernice. *Literacy Activities in Public Libraries*. Chicago: American Library Association, 1966.

Maddison, John. *Radio and Television in Literacy*. Paris: UNESCO, 1971.

Mezirow, Jack; Darkenwald, Gordon G.; and Knox, Alan B. *Last Gamble on Education*. Washington, D.C.: Adult Education Association, 1975.

Morris, Horace W. "They Are a Lost Generation." In *The New York Times*, Febr. 7, 1977.

The NALA Directory 1975–76. Syracuse, N.Y.: The National Affiliation for Literacy Advance, 1976.

National Advisory Council on Adult Education (NACAE). *A Target Population in Adult Education*. Washington, D.C.: U.S. Government Printing Office, 1974.

National Advisory Council on Adult Education (NACAE). *Beyond the Verge*. Section 1. Washington, D.C.: U.S. Government Printing Office, 1977a.

National Advisory Council on Adult Education (NACAE). *Futures and Amendments: Survey of State Support*. Section 2. Washington, D.C.: U.S. Government Printing Office, 1977b.

NCES. See *The Condition of Education*.

The New York Times. "Illegal Aliens." May 1, 1977a.

The New York Times. "New York Is Lowest in Youth Employment." Aug. 2, 1977b.

Nickse, Ruth S. "The Central New York External High School Diploma Program." In *Phi Delta Kappan*. October 1975a.

Nickse, Ruth S. *Development of a Performance Assessment System for the Central New York External High School Diploma Program: An Educational Alternative for Adults*. Syracuse, N.Y.: Regional Learning Service of Central New York, 1975b.

Nickse, Ruth S. *A Report on Adult Learners: A Profile of Fifty Adult Learners*. Syracuse, N.Y.: Syracuse Research Corporation, January 1976.

Olson, David R. "A Review of *Toward a Literate Society*, edited by Carroll and Chall." Reprinted from *Proceedings of the National Academy of Education*, Vol. 2, 1975.

Open Education for the People. A Report by the Educational Broadcasting Corporation to the City of New York on the Use of Broadcasting to Maximize Educational Opportunity. New York: Educational Broadcasting Corporation, April 1976.

Parker, James. "Competency-Based Adult Education Profile and Related Resources." (Draft.) Washington, D.C.: Division of Adult Education, U.S. Office of Education, 1976.

Participation in Adult Education 1975. Washington, D.C.: National Center for Education Statistics, forthcoming.

Patten, T. H., and Clark, C. E., Jr. "Literacy Training of Hard-Core Unemployed Negroes in Detroit." In *Journal of Human Resources*, Vol. 2, 1968, pp. 25–36.

Persell, Caroline Hodges. *Education and Inequality*. New York: The Free Press, 1977.

Policies and Procedures Handbook. Syracuse, N.Y.: Literacy Volunteers of America, 1975.

Public Broadcasting and Education; Report of the Task Force on Adult Education. Advisory Council of National Organizations to the Corporation for Public Broadcasting. Washington, D.C.: Corporation for Public Broadcasting, 1975.

"Questions and Answers about the Fortune Society Tutoring Program." Information sheet. New York: n.d.

Quitman County Center for Learning and Educational Development: Final Project Report. West Point, Miss.: Mary Holmes College; Marks, Miss.: Quitman Centers for Learning, 1970. ERIC ED 101 063.

Report of the North Carolina Conference to the Division of Adult Education Program. Washington, D.C.: U.S. Office of Education, 1970.

Resnick, Daniel P., and Resnick, Lauren B. "The Nature of Literacy: An Historical Exploration." In *Harvard Educational Review*, Vol. 47, No. 3, August 1977.

"Revolting Development: An Exchange with Ivan Illich." In *World Education REPORTS*, No. 14. New York: World Education, 1977.

Rosenthal, Edgar Lee. "Testimony Regarding Lifetime Learning Act." In *Lifetime Learning Act, 1975*. Hearing Before the Committee on Labor and Public Welfare. U.S. Senate, 94th Cong., Dec. 18, 1975. Washington: U.S. Government Printing Office, 1976.

Roy, Prodipto, and Kapoor, J. M. *The Retention of Literacy*. Delhi: Macmillan Company of India, Ltd., 1975.

Rubin, Lillian Breslow. *Worlds of Pain*. New York: Basic Books, 1976.

Ryan, T. A., and Furlong, William. "Literacy Programs in Industry, the Armed Forces, and Penal Institutions." In *Toward a Literate Society*, John B. Carroll and Jeanne Chall, eds. New York: McGraw-Hill Book Company, 1975.

Scribner, Sylvia, and Cole, Michael. *Literacy Without Schooling: Testing for Intellectual Effects*. Vai Literacy Project, Working Paper No. 2. New York: Rockefeller University, April 1978.

Seifer, Nancy. *Absent from the Majority: Working Class Women in America*. New York: The American Jewish Committee, 1973.

Sheehan, Susan. *A Welfare Mother*. Boston: Houghton-Mifflin, 1976.

Sheffield, James. *Retention of Literacy and Basic Skills*. New York: World Bank, 1977.

Society for the Preservation of Weeksville and Bedford-Stuyvesant History. Brochure prepared by the Weeksville Society. Brooklyn, N.Y.: n.d.

Special Labor Force Report No. 186. Washington, D.C.: U.S. Bureau of Labor Statistics, 1976.

Srinivasan, Lyra. "The Changing Situation—ABE and the World." Address delivered at the Consultation on Literacy/Adult Basic Education in the 1980s, sponsored by Intermedia at Stony Point, New York, March 1977a.

Srinivasan, Lyra. *Perspectives in Nonformal Adult Learning*. New York: World Education, 1977b.

Stauffer, John. *The NALA Study*. A Description of the National Affiliation for Literacy Advance. Syracuse, N.Y.: New Readers Press, 1973.

Stevens, Jenny. "The BBC Adult Literacy Project." In *Convergence*, Vol. 10, No. 1, 1977.

Sticht, T. G., ed. *Reading for Working: A Functional Literacy Anthology*. Alexandria, Va.: Human Resources Research Organization, 1975. ERIC ED 102 532.

Sticht, T. G., et al. *HumRRO's Literacy Research for the U.S. Army: Progress and Prospects*. Alexandria, Va.: HumRRO's Professional Paper 2–73, January 1973.

Sticht, T. G.: Caylor, J. S.; Kern, R. P.; and Fox, L. C. "Project REALISTIC: Determination of Adult Functional Literacy Levels." *Reading Research Quarterly*, Vol. 7, 1972, pp. 424–465.

Survival School System. St. Paul: American Indian Movement, 1974.

Theobald, Robert. *Beyond Despair*. Washington, D.C.: New Republic Book Co., 1976.

Thompson, Marguerite. "Developing a Positive Self-Image in the Inner City Minority Child Through the Use of the Community as a Classroom/ Weeksville." Ph.D. dissertation. Walden School of Advanced Studies, University of Rhode Island, 1976.

Training in Adult Literacy Schemes. London: Adult Literacy Resource Agency, n.d.

UNESCO. *Statement of the International Committee of Experts on Literacy*. Paris: 1962.

U.S. Bureau of Labor Statistics. See *Special Labor Force Reports*.

Weintraub, Bernard. "Navy Recruiting Is Hampered by Illiteracy." In *The New York Times*, Dec, 8, 1977.

Wirtz, Willard, and the National Manpower Institute. *The Boundless Resource*. A Prospectus for an Education-Work Policy. Washington, D.C.: New Republic Book Co., 1975.

Ziegler, Warren L. *On Civic Literacy*. Unpublished draft paper, 1974.

Ziegler, Warren L. "Who Benefits from Illiteracy? A Radical Critique of the Client Society." Presented as a Symposium on Adult Functional Literacy, 104th Annual Forum, National Conference on Social Welfare, 1977.

APPENDIX A

❦

Summary of Recommendations

Principal Conclusion. A major shift in national educational policy is needed to serve the educational needs of disadvantaged adults.

Principal Overall Recommendation. We recommend the establishment of new, pluralistic, community-based initiatives whose specific objective will be to serve the *most* disadvantaged hardcore poor, the bulk of whom never enroll in any existing program.

Specific Recommendation 1. The principal overall recommendation for community-based approaches to the most educationally disadvantaged adults should be given wide dissemination through the distribution of this study to legislators and policymakers, government officials, corporations and foundations, adult education professionals and practitioners, and those in other disciplines who are concerned with community development. The goal is to invite response and, where possible, support cooperation for the implementation of both the principal and the specific recommendations.

Specific Recommendation 2. A series of well-publicized regional conferences should be planned and held to gather data and to create a climate for understanding and implementing the central proposal for new community-based approaches.

Specific Recommendation 3. The persons who take part in the

133

regional conferences (Recommendation 2) should develop appropriate means within their own geographic areas to:
- increase public awareness of the situation and needs of marginal communities in their locales;
- involve other educators and service professionals in direct contacts with community people around the same concerns addressed in the original conferences;
- encourage the preparation of concept papers on the social context of literacy based on this experience; and
- begin to compile an inventory of successful community-based programs already going on in their area.

Specific Recommendation 4. A more systematic and accurate data-base about the groups, communities, and general population with which we are concerned should be developed and widely disseminated in diverse forms appropriate to the multiplicity of potential users.

Specific Recommendation 5. A consultation should be arranged to bring together those most active in relevant research efforts to exchange information and plan together for other needed research.

Specific Recommendation 6. As answers to the questions suggested under Recommendation 4 become available, and as regional groups begin to develop information about communities where successful programs are underway, several case studies should be undertaken to provide information about:
- past and present experience in the successful integration of community development and adult education goals;
- different models of financing these programs and information about levels of funding necessary for minimum and maximum accomplishment for different kinds of programs;
- alternative approaches that provide flexibility and freedom for indigenous groups to accomplish their own goals;
- a variety of mechanisms for integrated local planning and management of projects that cut across traditional lines of functional responsibility—community development, health services, education, job training, and the like;
- a list of competencies that community members believe are necessary for the full participation of their own members to assume greater responsibility for community life; and

• strategies for maintaining programs free of political control by self-selected "managers" from inside or outside the community.

Specific Recommendation 7. Educational agencies and organizations should be encouraged and enabled by appropriate funding to establish a number of pilot projects to test the hypotheses of this study and others emanating from work carrying out the earlier recommendations.

Specific Recommendation 8. A national commission on community-based initiatives should be established to provide visibility for the recommended new approaches and to provide leadership in the accomplishment of those tasks that *must* be done nationally. These tasks might include:
• the formulation and recommendation of policy proposals necessary to institutionalize community-based approaches;
• the writing of recommendations for legislation to implement the policies;
• the drafting of proposals to secure public funding;
• the education of the public about the significance of the new approaches to communities; and
• communication of experimental and research findings to professionals and practitioners.

Specific Recommendation 9. Background studies should be undertaken and alternative proposals tested to determine the most effective ways to obtain legislation and funding necessary if the new approaches are to be implemented nationally on a scale commensurate with the need.

Specific Recommendation 10. Citizen groups should be encouraged and enabled to address questions of social purpose and direction through the provision of concrete issue-oriented resource materials and agenda items about specific problem areas and illustrations. At the same time, these resource materials and agenda items should be oriented toward the construction of new options for the future.

Specific Recommendation 11. There should be instruments for social planning at the national level comparable to those that exist for economic planning.

APPENDIX B

✑

Acknowledgments

Carman Hunter of World Education has had primary responsibility for the planning, carrying out, and writing of this study. She has worked in association with David Harman of the Hebrew University of Jerusalem, who has been consultant to the project.

Debra Bloom of Harvard University provided research assistance. Martha Keehn, publications director of World Education, who prepared Chapter II, was fortunate to secure the advice of Tomas Frejka of the Population Council and Dr. D. D. Joshi of Agra University about the presentation of the statistical data. The publications staff at World Education—Martha Keehn, Margaret Brehmer, Joyce Rubin, and Hazel Westney—edited the first drafts of the paper. Karla M. Kaynee prepared the graphics for Chapter II.

The following persons not only read the paper and proffered their critical response, but also assembled for a day of consultation that focused on the recommendations that might grow out of the data presented in the first four chapters: Teca Raposo Greathouse, Brazilian educator; David Hargreaves, British Broadcasting Corporation; Don Miller, CEMREL; Leon Modeste, New York Urban League; David R. Olson, Ontario Institute for Studies in Education; Roberto Pérez Díaz, Barrio Education Project; Seth Spaulding, University of Pittsburgh; and Thomas Sticht, National Institute of Education. We assume responsibility for any errors of omission or commission as well as for the final formulation of the recommendations, but we acknowledge gratefully our heavy indebtedness to each of these persons. They sharpened our focus, pointed out inconsistencies, and supplied a fresh critical viewpoint.

We are beholden as well to those others who gave generously of their time and wisdom, in correspondence or conversation. All are listed here, but we would like to note here our appreciation to Paul Delker of the U.S. Office of Education and Jack Mezirow of Teachers College, Columbia University, for their insights into and sensitivity toward the special problems of the disadvantaged in our society.

The Ford Foundation made possible the preparation and publication of this study and World Education's worldwide experience provided the perspective. We wish to express our special thanks to Gail Spangenberg, the Foundation's program officer for the project, for her encouragement and support and to Tom Keehn, president of World Education, for his far-sightedness in perceiving the issue and how it related to international concerns and his determination to see the project to fruition.

We are delighted that the Ford Foundation selected Daniel Stein to edit the final document. His editorial skills and keen grasp of the field were invaluable. Most of all, we are grateful for the opportunity we have had to prepare this report on illiteracy in the United States. It has enabled us to focus on what clearly is an emerging issue.

PERSONS CONSULTED IN THE PREPARATION OF THIS PAPER

The following people generously answered questions and offered suggestions on the basis of their knowledge and experience.

Sally Allen
Educational Commission of the States
Denver, Colorado

Fred Bedell
N.Y. State Division for Youth
New York, New York

Hal Beder
Graduate School of Education
Rutgers University
New Brunswick, New Jersey

J. Herman Blake
Oakes College
University of California at
Santa Cruz

Ruth Boaz
National Center for
Educational Statistics
Washington, D.C.

Douglas Bodwell
Corporation for Public
Broadcasting
Washington, D.C.

James Broschart
U.S. Office of Education
Washington, D.C.

Robert Calvert
National Center for
Educational Statistics
Washington, D.C.

Robert Caswell
Laubach Literacy
Syracuse, New York

Jeanne Chall
Harvard University
Cambridge, Massachusetts

Barbara Chandler
U.S. Office of Education
Washington, D.C.

Septima Clark
Southern Christian Leadership
Council
Charleston, South Carolina

Yehezekiel Cohen
Academy of Sciences
Israel

Ruth Colvin
Literacy Volunteers of America
Syracuse, New York

Frank Corrigan
National Center for Education
Statistics
Washington, D.C.

Jinx Crouch
Literacy Volunteers of America
Syracuse, New York

Lloyd David
Cambridge University
Cambridge, England

Walter Davis
Education Director
AFL-CIO
Washington, D.C.

Paul Delker
U.S. Office of Education
Washington, D.C.

W.A. Devereux
Adult Literacy Resource
Agency
London, England

James Dorland
National Association for Adult
and Continuing Education
Washington, D.C.

Rosemary Durant
Henry Street Settlement
House/Urban Life Center
New York, New York

James Durham
Native American Solidarity
Committee
New York, New York

Gary Eyre
National Advisory Council on
Adult Education
Washington, D.C.

George Eyster
Appalachian Adult Education
Center
Morehead, Kentucky

Ann Gael
Native American Solidarity
Committee
New York, New York

Jane Garmey
WNET/13
New York, New York

Madonna Gilbert
We Will Remember Survival
School
Rapid City, South Dakota

P.T. Gorman
University of Essex
Essex, England

William Griffith
University of Chicago
Chicago, Illinois

Connie Haendle
Literacy Volunteers of America
Syracuse, New York

Robert Hall
U.S. Office of Education
Washington, D.C.

William Harley
National Association for
Educational TV
Washington, D.C.

Grace Healey
Civic Literacy Project
Syracuse, New York

Thomas Hill
Right to Read
Washington, D.C.

Dianne Kangisser
Literacy Volunteers of America
New York, New York

Michele Korf
WNET/13
New York, New York

Shulamit Kotek
Adult Education Association
Israel

Jonathan Kozol
Boston, Massachusetts

Martha Lane
Lutheran Church Women
Volunteer Reading Aides
Philadelphia, Pa.

Linda Lehman-Hill
Regional Learning Services
Syracuse, New York

Pat Lein
Regional Learning Services
Syracuse, New York

Dana Lichty
Bronx Community College
New York, New York

Robert Luke
Adult Education Association
Washington, D.C.

Helene Mallett
ABE Teacher
Long Island, New York

Olive Mann
Literacy Project Referral
Service
British Broadcasting
Corporation
London, England

Joan Maynard
Weeksville Project
Brooklyn, New York

Naomi McIntosh
Open University
Milton Keynes, England

Constance McQueen
New York City Community
College
Brooklyn, New York

John E. Merritt
Open University
Milton Keynes, England

Jack Mezirow
Teachers College
Columbia University
New York, New York

Roy Miller
Brooklyn Public Library
Brooklyn, New York

Andres Montes
Right to Read
Washington, D.C.

Cathy Moorhouse
Inner London Education
Authority
London, England

Ruth Nickse
National Institute of Education
Washington, D.C.

Norvell Northcutt
APL Project
University of Texas at Austin

Amos Odenyo
Department of Sociology
City University of New York
York College, New York

Michael O'Keefe
Department of Health,
Education and Welfare
Washington, D.C.

Michael Parer
Indiana University
Bloomington, Indiana

Roberto Pérez Díaz
Barrio Education Project
San Antonio, Texas

Colin Pointer
Kensington Adult Education
Institute
London, England

Jovelino Ramos
National Council of Churches
New York, New York

Jane Root
Literacy Volunteers of America
Syracuse, New York

Edward Lee Rosenthal
Rutgers Labor Center
Rutgers University
New Brunswick, New Jersey

Mina Shaughnessy
City University of New York
New York, New York

Elaine Sheldon
APL Project
University of Texas at Austin

Adelaide Silvia
National Association for
Literacy Advancement
Laubach Literacy
Syracuse, New York

Peter Simmons
Kirschner Associates, Inc.
Washington, D.C.

Marshall Smith
National Institute of Education
Washington, D.C.

Arthur Stock
National Institute of Adult
Education
Leicester, England

Jessie Ulin
National Association for Adult
and Continuing Education
Washington, D.C.

John Villaume
Harvard University
Cambridge, Massachusetts

Betty Ward
Adult Education Association
Washington, D.C.

Phyllis Weaver
Harvard University
Cambridge, Massachusetts

William Wilson
Kentucky Educational
Television
Lexington, Kentucky

Roger Yarrington
American Association of
Community and Junior Colleges
Washington, D.C.

Kalman Yaron
Martin Buber Center of Adult
Education
Hebrew University
Jerusalem, Israel

Warren Ziegler
Syracuse University
Syracuse, New York

APPENDIX C

A Selected Annotated Bibliography

prepared by
Carman Hunter

with the assistance of
Debra Bloom

INTRODUCTION

❧

Earlier we referred to this study as an archaeological expedition. Each person we consulted sent us to someone else; each writer suggested additional material. After the conclusion of our work, we were persuaded to return to the material that had influenced our thinking, in order to construct a bibliography that would serve as a record of our journey.

The result is not a comprehensive bibliography on literacy and illiteracy. Excluded are significant studies from the Third World where much of the seminal research has taken place. Excluded, also, are some important studies from the U.S. on linguistics, reading, and cognitive development. This bibliography does not have an exclusive focus on literacy. Rather, in its totality it seeks to present the relationship between illiteracy on the one hand and poverty, discrimination, and the powerlessness of certain identifiable groups on the other. Our list of references emphasizes the choices facing the society in its approach to the most neglected groups within it rather than the technical aspects of teaching adults to read or to acquire functional skills.

If this selected bibliography has any merit, it is because it brings together material on the social context of adult illiteracy; on the changing concepts of literacy; on various inconclusive efforts to measure literacy; on the inevitable relation between the most severe instances of educational disadvantage and all of the other major social and economic forms of disadvantage; and on social criticism that seeks new models for the future.

Section 1 of this selected bibliography contains an alphabetical listing of materials bearing on all of these aspects of the present situation in the U.S. The notations below each item describe its significance for this study. They do not attempt to present the total argument of the writer.

A second section is appended to the general bibliography. It contains a representative sampling of existing experimentation, studies, and curriculum materials related to present programs. The section is subdivided into the following categories:

A. Demonstration projects, methods, and evaluation
B. Teachers and paraprofessionals: materials for training
C. Recruitment and retention
D. Curriculum materials
E. Bibliographies of curriculum materials
F. The use of broadcast media

Section 2 is an addendum to the main bibliography which, by its sheer size, indicates the weight of attention that has been given to working within existing programmatic structures. Some of the experimentation has produced data that, if applied to ABE (Adult Basic Education) programs, could result in positive improvements.

Our conclusions, however, as recorded in the main body of the study, suggest that more comprehensive approaches must be sought if adults who are not now served by these programs are to be reached. The number of programs described here that address the needs of the poor in the context of the communities where they live and work is exceedingly small. A closer alignment between community development and education is urgently needed. Comprehensive, community-based alternatives to traditional schooling will emerge if research and experimentation go beyond the boundaries of education as these boundaries are commonly defined.

SECTION 1

Adult Education in Community Organizations 1972. By Evelyn Kay. Washington, D.C.: National Center for Educational Statistics, U.S. Office of Education, 1974.

A brief statistical survey of the nearly 67,000 community organizations that offered 321,000 adult courses to some 11 million participants in 1972. These are private, nonprofit organizations, including churches and other religious organizations, Y's and Red Cross chapters, civic and social service organizations, and cultural and social groups.

Adult Functional Competency: A Report to the Office of Education Dissemination Review Panel. Austin, Texas: Division of Extension, University of Texas, 1975.

and

Adult Functional Competency: A Summary. Austin, Texas: Division of Extension, University of Texas, 1975.

These two publications report the objectives, theory, methodology, and results of the adult performance level study (APL) carried out by the University of Texas at Austin for the U.S. Office of Education. The validity and reliability of the study are defended. Implications for adult education and adult basic education are drawn and some activities and products indicated for ABE are described. APL goals and tasks are described. These have become the basis for the APL testing program and for curriculum development and teacher-training.

Bazany, M., Badizadegan, M., Kaufmann, H. D., and Khosrowshahi, K. *Registration, Participation and Attendance in Functional Literacy Courses*. Esfahan: Work-Oriented Adult Literacy Pilot Project in Iran, Evaluation Studies No. 2, 1970.

and

Bazany, M., Kaufmann, H. D., and Safavi, A. *Demographic Characteristics and Interest in Participation in Functional Literacy Courses*, Esfahan: Work-Oriented Adult Literacy Pilot Project in Iran, Evaluation Studies No. 4, 1970.

and

Bazany, M. *Work-Oriented Adult Literacy in Iran: An Experiment: Analysis, Optimalization and Comparisons of the Method*. Vol. 6, Final Technical Report. Esfahan, Iran: 1973.

These three reports describe research conducted in Iran in relation to its Experimental World Literacy Program. They provide information regarding participant, nonparticipant, and dropout characterizations and motivations and conclude that, where a "literacy consciousness" is not culturally normative, there is little likelihood that literacy skills will be learned and functionally retained.

Beitz, Charles, and Washburn, Michael. *Creating the Future: A Guide to Living and Working for Social Change*. New York: Bantam Books, 1974.

This book is based on the assumption that every citizen has an obligation to help create the future in both personal and sociopolitical areas. It stresses building institutions and movements for peace, world order, and ecological controls—all for the development of a global society. It is a call for a new world order to which the common people of all regions of the world can contribute.

Berger, Peter L., and Neuhaus, Richard J. *To Empower People: The Role of Mediating Structures in Public Policy*. Washington, D.C.: American Enterprise Institute for Public Policy Research, 1977.

The initial report of a project to explore the role of alternative structures in providing welfare-state services. The structures considered (neighborhood, family, church, and voluntary associations) could, in the view of the authors, legitimize needed services and provide them in acceptable, democratic ways, thus reducing dependence on government bureaucracies. They stress the salutary strength of pluralism as a means of resisting totalitarian tendencies in policy-planning and implementation. They call for strong resistance to "massification" and the encouragement of a new empowerment of citizens.

Best, Fred, and Stern, Barry. *Lifetime Distribution of Education, Work, and Leisure: Research, Speculations, and Policy Implications*. Washington, D.C.: Institute for Educational Leadership, Post-secondary Education Convening Authority, 1976.

Describes the increase of "nonwork time" at the earliest and latest stages of life and raises questions about whether work, leisure, and education should be part of a cyclic rather than a linear pattern in our life-span. The authors relate this question to the number one U.S. problem—the shortage of jobs except in time of war—and the resulting social problems—an expensive, degrading welfare system, crime, mental illness—problems borne disproportionately by minorities, women, youth, and older people. They look also at the unequal distribution of leisure and education and note that economic opportunity is a better predictor of educational attainment than vice versa. They call for drastic change in the distribution of work, leisure, and education across different population groups, discuss some of the proposals for accomplishing this goal, and conclude that the cyclic pattern offers most promise. Within their proposal is the assumption that the job-shortage problems may continue and, therefore, the solution would involve giving everyone more time for work and education, so that jobs could be more widely distributed.

Blaug, M. "Literacy and Economic Development." In *The School Review*, 1966, Vol. 74, pp. 394–418.

Blaug concludes that "while literacy may not always cure poverty, affluence always eradicates illiteracy," and thereby refutes the contention that literacy is a sure way to attain economic development.

Bormuth, John R. "Reading Literacy: Its Definition and Assessment." In *Reading Research Quarterly*, Vol. 9, No. 1, 1973–74.
  Bormuth makes the point that literacy has to do not only with how a person can obtain maximum value from the materials he needs to read but also his ability to exhibit socially appropriate reading behavior—to respond appropriately to *all* reading tasks.

Bowles, Samuel, and Gintis, Herbert. *Schooling in Capitalist America.* New York: Basic Books, Inc., 1976.
  The authors pose a socialist alternative as the only road to educational and economic reform of sufficient magnitude to meet the challenges and contradictions inherent in present systems. They propose steps toward economic democracy, to be initiated now by conscious educational reforms that would embrace the needs of the working class poor.

Brickman, William W., and Lehrer, Stanley. *Education and the Many Faces of the Disadvantaged.* New York: John Wiley and Sons, Inc., 1972.
  The focus of this collection of essays is on the role of the schools in changing the situation of disadvantaged children through equal educational opportunities. Most essays were previously published in *School and Society* and cover a broad range of the disadvantaged—inner-city and rural poor, black and Spanish-speaking Americans, Native Americans, immigrants, and refugees. Efforts to improve schooling through innovative programs and better teacher-training are described. While the essays vary in quality, the whole collection reflects the faith that through greater cultural sensitivity on the part of teachers and administrators, through remedial programs and slow, consistent attention to the problems, solutions will be found within the system of schooling as it exists. The editors and essayists suggest that educators can "remove the barriers that divide humanity into the advantaged and disadvantaged."

Broschart, James R. *A Synthesis of Selected Manuscripts about the Education of Adults in the United States.* Prepared for the Bureau of Occupational and Adult Education. Washington, D.C.: U.S. Office of Education, 1976.
  This draft document was published by HEW in 1977 under the title *Lifelong Learning in the Nation's Third Century.* It provides a comprehensive survey of the literature and current thinking on adult education, including learning theory, practice, delivery systems, and funding. The focus is on life-long learning as a concept and a practical struggle to move to a situation where learning from cradle to grave is a norm.

Burke, Richard, and Chiappetta, Michael. *Characteristics of Illiterates and Program Hypotheses*. Final Report to United States Agency for International Development/Technical Assistance, May 4, 1977.

　　In dealing with rural populations, the distinction between literates and illiterates is relatively unimportant. Productive economic activities may foster a need for literacy, but it is not always demonstrable that literacy will foster productive economic activities.

Carroll, John B., and Chall, Jeanne, *Toward a Literate Society*. New York: McGraw-Hill, Inc., 1975.

　　The book contains a series of papers commissioned by the Committee on Reading of the National Academy of Education. The Committee was appointed in response to initiatives of the then–U.S. Commissioner of Education, the late James E. Allen, Jr., whose commitment to the discovery of new approaches to teaching of reading had resulted in the Right to Read program. Three of the papers are of central interest and are mentioned separately in this bibliography, as is the extensive analysis by David R. Olson of the total contents of the volume and of the Right to Read program itself. The three chapters are; "Adult Illiteracy in the U.S.," by Rose-Marie Weber; "Literacy Programs in Industry, the Armed Forces, and Penal Institutions," by T. A. Ryan and William Furlong; and "Political Implications of a National Reading Effort," by Natalie Saxe and Richard H. DeLone.

Challenges: The Commission on Adult Basic Education. News, Highlights, and Challenges for Adult Basic Education. Manhattan, Kans.: Adult Education, Summer 1976.

　　John A. Niemi comments on the major difficulties encountered by middle-class ABE teachers working with the educationally disadvantaged poor who reject currently available programs as inappropriate to their needs. He calls for further research into the nature of the many culturally different groups from which ABE students come.

Charnofsky, Stanley. *Educating the Powerless*. Belmont, Calif.: Wadsworth Publishing Co., Inc., 1971.

　　The author deals with the powerlessness that pervades the lifestyles of the poor. His chief concern is for the discovery of new educational approaches to the children of the poor, who, he suggests, are powerless because they are different and, for this reason, made to feel inferior. He does not want to change the child, but, rather, to alter the system. He describes a humanistic curriculum model and teaching modes that emphasize the facilitator role. Many of his descriptions of the condition of powerlessness and his prescriptions for programs are closely related to the concerns of this study, despite the focus on children rather than adults.

Childers, Thomas, assisted by Post, Joyce A. *The Information-Poor in America*. Metuchen, N.J.: The Scarecrow Press, Inc., 1975.
This book is the final report of a study entitled "Knowledge/Information Needs of the Disadvantaged." It contains an extensive bibliography of documents related to the information needs, communication patterns, and information-seeking behavior of disadvantaged Americans. The bibliography is also arranged by major topics—including, among others, employment, education, health, housing, and welfare. Not only is the bibliography useful for background regarding the disadvantaged, but the introductory chapters that describe the search, define terms, and comment on areas of need are extremely helpful. Chapter 5, "Who are the Information-Poor?" is particularly enlightening in its presentation of the disadvantaged and the way in which the society sees them—as reflected in the literature. Needed research is pointed out by the authors.

Clearinghouse for Community Based Free Standing Educational Institutions, *Newsletter*. Washington, D.C.: published 2 or 3 times a year by CBFSEI.
The *Newsletter* and other CBFSEI publications reflect the interests of a network of member organizations that focus on the relation between community organization and education. Created after work on this study was completed, the Clearinghouse addresses the issues that were central to the conclusions and recommendations of the study.

Cole, Michael. "How Education Affects the Mind." In *Human Nature*, April 1978.
The author presents data from research projects—in Liberia, Mexico, and Guatemala—regarding intellectual development resulting from schooling. He concludes that although schools may possibly produce general intellectual change, it is more probable that commonly used tests measure only the success of schools in transmitting specific skills required by education itself. He concludes that indiscriminate requirement of a high school diploma or a college degree as a prerequisite for employment is probably not justified. The lack of correlation between the kinds of skills transmitted by schools and the requirements of many jobs should be adjusted so that schools will prepare persons for the requirements of adult living. He remarks on the difficulty of achieving such a balance, because for many education is the one variable in their lives that can be controlled. Others, like social class, one's parents' education, ethnicity, and nutrition, are accidents of birth.

And so the myths supporting education as it is will probably prevail.

Coles, Gerald S. "U.S. Literacy Statistics: How to Succeed With Hardly Trying." In *Literacy Work*, Vol. 15, No. 2, Summer 1976, pp. 47–68.

Among the points brought out in this article are: (1) that census-takers ask about one's ability to read and write only when the interviewee has less than a seventh grade education, so the Census Bureau underestimates the extent of illiteracy in the U.S., (2) these statistics are inadequate for understanding the poor, (3) literacy rates have dropped faster than the number of literacy programs have increased.

Coles, Robert. "Work and Self-Respect." In *Daedalus*, Vol. 105, No. 4, Fall 1976.

A report based on the author's first-hand acquaintance with workers and their families. He describes how they perceive adulthood or maturity, contrasting their perceptions with those of middle class and intellectual groups. He remarks on their "fierce pride, shrewd realism, and insistent rejection of self-pity, or the pity of others." He further points out the close relationship between personal identity and work, which gives a sense of worth and self-respect. In this context he evaluates the psychologically devastating effects of unemployment on the working class.

Collins, Randall. "Some Comparative Principles on Educational Stratification." In *Harvard Educational Review*, Vol. 47, No. 1, February 1977.

An argument demonstrating three sources of demand for education: the demands of the individual for practical skills, the desire of groups for social solidarity and high status, and the concern of nation-states for effective political control. These sources and their consequences operate within a market for cultural goods that behaves much like the market for economic goods.

Community Education. Appalachian Adult Education Center, Final Report. Morehead, Ky.: Morehead University, 1975.

The report of a demonstration project to spell out directions for improving adult education in rural and small-town settings. Based on careful analysis of rural and small-town cultural and economic realities, the report urges that the educational needs of persons of all ages be coordinated within the community, relying on community resources with the goal of improving the quality of individual and community life. It calls for cross-generational, cross-community efforts based on local cultural traditions. It advocates local community-planning sessions, in-service training of community personnel, and ongoing evaluation by the community.

The Condition of Education. A Statistical Report on the Condition of American Education. Washington, D.C.: U.S. Government Printing Office, 1975.

and

The Condition of Education. A Statistical Report on the Condition of American Education together with A Description of the Activities of the National Center for Educational Statistics, 1976. Washington, D.C.: NCES, U.S. Office of Education, March 1976.

These yearly reports of the National Center for Educational Statistics provide a useful and continually updated statistical framework within which educators and policy-makers can consider educational practice. While the focus is primarily on formal schooling, much relevant data are pulled together that have bearings on adult illiteracy in the United States. The 1976 edition includes a section comparing education in the U.S. with other countries. Fully illustrated with graphics and tables.

Coombs, Philip H., et al. *New Paths to Learning for Rural Children and Youth*. New York: International Council for Educational Development, 1973.

An examination of what might be done through nonformal education to help meet the minimum essential learning needs of educationally deprived children in the developing world. Contains useful discussion and definitions of formal, informal, and nonformal education.

Current Population Reports. Washington, D.C.: U.S. Bureau of the Census, 1976.

Monthly up-dates of U.S. census information.

Daugat, Sam V., and Daugat, Jo Ann. "Literacy in Quest of a Definition." In *Convergence*, Vol. 10, No. 1, 1977.

An essay exploring diverse routes toward a definition of literacy. The authors conclude that literacy implies the ability to use language as a tool; that one of the major objectives of literacy is freedom from social, economic, and political impotence; and, finally, that literacy is a changing concept and depends both on where one starts and where one wants to go.

The Experimental World Literacy Program: A Critical Assessment. Compiled by the Secretariats of UNESCO and UNDP. Paris: UNESCO Press, 1976.

In 1966 UNESCO and UNDP embarked on a major effort to evolve an effective approach toward overcoming illiteracy. It was an attempt to examine the relationship between literacy and development by demonstrating the economic and social returns of literacy. *A Critical Assessment* is the final report of this effort. It describes briefly the 11 experimental projects and makes an analysis and critique. One of the most significant questions raised is whether established institutions can accept the actual exercise of newly acquired skills, it being evident that their exercise presupposes far-reaching change. The effort to establish linkages between literacy training and functional training yielded few models.

Fisher, Donald L. *Functional Literacy and the Schools*. Washington, D.C.: National Institute of Education, 1978.

As the title suggests, the primary concern of this study is to assess the effectiveness of the schools in literacy training. The author, after analyzing the findings of all the major studies of adult literacy, concludes that the situation is far less bleak than reactions to the studies—in the press and official educational circles—suggest. He offers several ways of reinterpreting the findings and concludes that *"few if any functional illiterates were actually awarded high school diplomas."* He pays scant attention to those who fail to graduate from high school, among whom, he says, the bulk of the illiterates are found. The author is confident that the rising rate of high school completion among all subgroups in the population will increasingly improve the rate of literacy. He also asserts that, contrary to public opinion, it is unlikely that educational reform in recent years has had a negative effect on literacy rates.

Freire, Paulo. "The Adult Literacy Process as Cultural Action for Freedom." In the *Harvard Educational Review*, Vol. 40, No. 2, May 1970.

Freire writes from a Third World perspective, but with obvious implications for education in general. He rejects mechanistic conceptions of the adult literacy process, advocating instead a theory and practice based upon authentic dialogue between teachers and learners. Such dialogue, in Freire's approach, centers upon codified representations of the learners' existential situations and leads not only to their acquisition of literacy skills, but more importantly to their awareness of their right and capacity as human beings to transform reality. Becoming literate, then, means far more than learning to decode the written representation of a sound system. It is truly an act of knowing, through which people are able to look critically at the culture that has shaped them and to move toward reflection and positive action upon their world.

Freire, Paulo. *Pedagogy in Progress: The Letters to Guinea-Bissau*. New York: The Seabury Press, 1978.

Freire's social and educational theories regarding people's participation in creating their own future are applied to the problems of a small, newly independent nation in which 95 percent of the adult population is illiterate. Freire describes the cooperative efforts of an outside team and Guinea-Bissau's Ministry of Education in the slow, careful process of enlisting the peasant masses in cultural action for their own growth.

Froomkin, Joseph, and Wolfson, Robert. *Adult Education 1972, A Re-Analysis*. Washington, D.C.: Educational Policy and Research Center, 1977.
 The authors reexamine the 1972 NCES data and attempt to prove that educationally disadvantaged adults get a larger share of the "total contracted hours" in adult education than is assumed when only "participation" is measured. The argument is strained and the effort to say that the delivery of adult education is not as skewed to the rich as we have been led to believe seems hardly worth the effort.

Ginsburg, Helen. "Domestic Issue #1: Jobs for all the Jobless." *Christianity and Crisis*, Vol. 37, No. 22, Jan. 16, 1978.
 The author examines the impact of high levels of unemployment on the lives of blacks, youth, and women, already the economically weakest, most powerless, and most victimized by discrimination. She makes a plea for full employment as the foremost domestic human rights issue of our time and adds that, to secure it, political and social pressure must be mobilized, especially among the persons who suffer most, but are caught, at present, in the lethargy of hopelessness.

Glazer, Nathan. "Liberty, Equality, Fraternity and Ethnicity." In *Daedalus*, Vol. 105, No. 4, Fall 1976.
 The author deals with the difficult tensions between liberty and equality as these are felt in relation to social programs. He looks at the many difficulties of achieving equality in a multi-ethnic society and at the expansion of the concept of equality to include the expectation of *concrete* and *actual* equality. Some of the current explanations of inequality are explored as well as the phenomenon of a growing fear of any hypothesis regarding its origin. He calls for a realistic understanding that embraces difference but maintains the basic relationship of subgroups within the larger society.

Grebelsky, Ora, and Yaron, Kalman. "Trends in Adult Education in Israel." In *Lifelong Education in Israel*. Jerusalem, Israel: The Public Advisory Council on Adult Education, The Adult Education Association of Israel, The Israel National Commission for UNESCO, 1972.
 This essay is particularly interesting because of the approach taken in Israel to the diverse needs of new immigrants. Adult education is not artificially separated from the whole range of social, occupational, family, and personal needs, but is the coordinating force responding to all these needs. Volunteers are trained and used in basic community approaches. All of the gov-

ernmental agencies offer resources for what is perceived as an integrated effort.

Griffith, William S., et al. *Public Policy in Financing Basic Education for Adults*. An Investigation of the Cost-Benefit Relationships in Adult Basic Education in Public Schools and Community Colleges. Vol. 1, Summary and Recommendations. Chicago: Department of Education, The University of Chicago, May 1974.

The study was an effort to document the effects of federal financing of ABE on the delivery systems at the state and community levels and to propose models to optimize the extent and variety of adult education offerings for the public. Recommendations are made about organization, interagency and interinstitutional coordination of community resources, diversification of adult education offerings, and other relevant matters.

Griffith, William S., and Cervero, Ronald M. *The Adult Performance Level Program: A Serious and Deliberate Examination*. Address presented at Adult Education Act/National Advisory Council on Adult Education Convention, New York, November 1976.

A radical critique of the APL (Adult Performance Level) study, its conclusions, and the attention it has received. The authors suggest that the APL approach is not novel, and refer to several earlier educators to prove the point. They take exception to the lack of explanation of the values assumed by those who constructed the APL tests. They further assert that only sketchy evidence exists to support any claim that performance on these tests actually measures functional competence. They conclude that the whole APL effort will be commendable only if it results in the development of ABE programs that are more effective than existing programs.

Hamalian, Leo, and Karl, Frederick R., eds., *The Fourth World: The Imprisoned, The Poor, The Sick, The Elderly, and Underaged in America*. New York: Dell Publishing Co., 1976.

A collection of essays about and by the disadvantaged in U.S. society. The editors suggest that the "Fourth World" is made up of persons and groups who exist outside national politics and outside the economic system, related only marginally to the culture.

Harman, David. *Community Fundamental Education*. Lexington, Mass.: D. C. Heath and Co., 1974.

The author addresses literacy in the context of development, describing the theoretical relation of the two concepts and providing examples and references to research in the field. He presents a model of fundamental education as a coherent system rooted in the web of people's relationships and experiences in their communities. Literacy per se is not an overt objective, but an instrument within a program for change in the dynamic world of the participants.

Harman, David. "Illiteracy: An Overview." In *Harvard Educational Review*, Vol. 40, No. 2, May 1970.
    The writer reviews concepts of literacy and functional literacy and discusses their relationships to the scope of the problem and to attempts to remedy the condition of illiteracy. He argues that approaches to adults through adult basic education programs should be situation-specific and planned in relation to need rather than to attaining grade school equivalence.

Harman, David. "Illiteracy, Poverty, and Racism: Their Interconnection." Paper delivered at the National Conference on Social Welfare, Chicago, May 16, 1977.
    The author suggests that illiterates who are members of subgroups whose literacy levels are consistently low will seek literacy skills only as they engage in more activities demanding literacy and as literacy then becomes an important concept in their "cultural map." This, he says, is a cultural transformation, not simply an instructional task. He further stresses the need to approach each cultural group on its own turf in accordance with its own norms and definitions.

Harman, David. "Review of The Experimental World Literacy Program: A Critical Assessment." In *Harvard Educational Review*, Vol. 47, No. 3, August 1977.
    The author contends that despite constant references to the cultural, social, and economic context within which the various experimental programs occurred, the research design and mindset of at least some associated with local projects reflected unwarranted claims about the possible accomplishments of literary campaigns.

Harman, Willis W. *An Incomplete Guide to the Future*. San Francisco: San Francisco Book Company, 1976.
    A treatment of the dilemmas of technological-industrial society as it faces the future. Consideration is given to future research, growth, work roles, world distribution, control, changing images of humankind, the characteristics of the transindustrial future, and some possible strategies for the future.
    The author describes desirable changes in all sectors of the society: the public, or governmental sector, the private business sector, and the citizen, or voluntary sector. He sees the emergence of new possibilities for human life in response to the challenges presented both by diminishing resources and ethical sensibility.

Harris, Louis, and Associates. *The 1971 Reading Difficulty Index*. New York, 1971.

An exploration of respondents' ability to answer questions about newspaper employment ads. Ninety-two percent of all respondents got all nine of the questions correct. Only 70 percent of all blacks tested got nine correct.

Heilbroner, Robert L. *An Inquiry into the Human Prospect*. New York: W. W. Norton, 1974.

The author sees rapid population growth, obliterative weapons, and dwindling planetary resources as precursors of dangerous levels of international tension that will not abate unless there is either great increase in production in the Third World *or* massive redistribution of wealth from richer to poorer nations. He foresees both natural and social dangers to existence and sees little hope that either capitalist or socialist nations will sufficiently alter their life-styles to correspond with the changes demanded. He suggests that neither producers nor consumers will voluntarily abandon present industrial modes of development and fears the resulting inevitability of wars. Yet, at the same time, he urges intellectuals in Western nations to try to change attitudes and to call upon the fortitude of their fellow citizens in the interest of survival.

"Illiteracy in America." *Harvard Educational Review* (A Special Issue). Cambridge, Mass.: Harvard University, 1970.

The issue contains articles by Paulo Freire and David Harman; position papers by Neil Postman, Jane Torrey, and Wayne O'Neil; and a symposium whose participants were Jeanne Chall, David Harman, Ephraim Isaac, Dorothy Jones, Frank and Robert Laubach, and Wayne O'Neil, followed by a series of brief comments by other educators. The overview is helpful and raises many of the same issues still being considered: How is literacy more than reading? What is the relation between literacy and development? What are the social implications of literacy? The articles are uneven in their depth of treatment and approach to the problems.

Jencks, Christopher, et al. *Inequality. A Re-assessment of the Effect of Family and Schooling in America*. New York: Harper & Row, 1973.

A controversial look at the differences in academic achievement by different ethnic and social groups within the United States. Mr. Jencks and his colleagues study various aspects of inequality in education (access to opportunities, native ability, heredity, environmental pressures) and come up with some conclusions, particularly about the influence of family, that are being widely challenged. Appendixes give an analysis of the statistics and an extensive list of references.

Kahn, Herman, et al. *The Next 200 Years*. New York: William Morrow, 1976.

A response by Kahn and the Hudson Institute to the so-called prophets of doom, who suggest that unchecked technological and economic growth as understood in the West will deplete the planet's natural resources and create social upheaval, resulting in the destruction of life as we know it. Dr. Kahn instead predicts universal affluence and high standards of living throughout the world. He decries the impractical arguments of the intellectual elite and calls for the "socialization" of the children of the upper classes so that they can more gracefully accept affluence. He relies on the wisdom of the scientific community to monitor long-term problems. The book concludes with questions: What kind of a life will a genetically engineered, vital-organ-replaceable, mental-state-adjustable, computer-robot-assisted human being want to live? Who will direct and manipulate our future and to what ends? The future world will be one of abundance, decreased competition, and questions like those we now confront but in greatly increased range and magnitude. Dr. Kahn likes the prospect!

Keehn, Thomas B. "Development and Literacy Restated: Functional Education for Individual, Community, and National Development." Prepared for an international conference on Emerging Issues in Cultural Relations in an Interdependent World, East-West Center, Honolulu, December 9–10, 1976.

Traces the changes in the conceptualization of development from an exclusively economic focus to the inclusion of the broader aspects of personal and national growth and well-being. The author stresses the significant contribution of nonformal education, with its emphasis on personal and community needs, as a means of promoting human development in its most comprehensive sense. He describes approaches and methods of education that have evolved in the Third World and notes their applicability within the U.S.

Kirschner Associates, Inc. *Summary Report: An Analysis of Selected Issues in Adult Education*. Prepared for the Office of Planning, Budgeting and Evaluation. Washington, D.C.: U.S. Office of Education, February 1976.

Volume 1 discusses various types, populations, and facilities for adult education programs across the country and the demand for such programs. Volume 2 lists all federally funded projects. Volume 3 is an annotated bibliography.

After describing the potential population for currently available adult education programs, the authors provide a series of recommendations notable for their inclusiveness and lack of criteria for choosing among options, given the limited financing for publicly sponsored programs. It seems that everything should be a "public policy goal"—from literacy for all adults, high school education for all, job-related education, and adult functional education to education for personal development. They call for stress on education for women, minorities, the elderly, and the middle class. They do suggest careful examination of current legislation to ensure that lack of equity is overcome. They call for evaluation, research on effective recruitment techniques, on curricula for special groups, and the relating of credentials to competencies.

Knox, Alan B. *Adult Development and Learning*. San Francisco, Ca.: Jossey-Bass, 1977.

The author synthesizes the findings of over 1,000 recent studies of adult development and learning needs. He describes the circumstances under which adults learn most effectively, the ways in which learning ability is affected by age, by family roles, social activities, occupation, personality characteristics, and health. As a result of his extensive work, Knox calls attention to the fact that available studies reflect, almost exclusively, the experience of white middle-class Americans. He reports that only a few studies deal with the similarities and differences among adults from various social class levels.

Lewis, Oscar. *La Vida*. New York: Random House, 1968.

In this book Oscar Lewis, who had dealt with rural poverty in Latin America in *The Children of Sanchez* and *Four Men*, examines the lives of a Puerto Rican family in San Juan and their relatives in New York city.

The family being studied is the Rios family, consisting of five households, a mother and two married daughters in Puerto Rico and a married son and daughter in New York City. The family is a matriarchy, and the Rios women have been prostitutes for several generations.

Although the Rios family suffers the problems common to those in the culture of poverty, most notably physical and emotional ill-health, Lewis is "impressed by the strengths in this family . . . their fortitude, vitality, resilience, and ability to cope with problems which would paralyze many middle-class individuals."

Liebow, Elliot. *Tally's Corner: A Study of Negro Streetcorner Men*. Boston: Little, Brown and Co., 1967.

Liebow's study centers around the Carry Out Shop, which serves as an informal gathering place and communication center on a corner in the Washington, D.C., ghetto. He describes the lives of the men who gather there and the social structure of the streetcorner world, their friendships, family patterns, jobs. The men inhabit a world somewhere between that of the upwardly mobile, lower-middle-class, working man and that of the derelict. These men are "losers" who have not abdicated completely their quest for dignity. For more than a year Liebow frequented Tally's Corner and came to know the group he describes. He details the ways in which relationships between blacks and whites, the educated and uneducated, the poor and the nonpoor are mixed up with roles and acting. His account helps the reader understand something of the resiliency of these men in the face of the disorganization, insecurity, and anticommunity forces that operate in their lives.

Lifetime Learning Act, 1975. Hearing Before the Subcommittee on Education of the Committee on Labor and Public Welfare. U.S. Senate, 94th Cong., Dec. 18, 1975.

Despite the wording of the act, "lifetime learning means any program, project, activity, or service designed to meet the changing educational needs of Americans throughout their lives, and includes, but is not limited to, adult basic education, continuing education, or remedial education or special education for individuals with special needs, job training programs and preretirement and postretirement training and education programs for the elderly." The speakers said very little about education below the postsecondary level. One gets the impression that educators and the agencies they represent are more interested in the potential economic benefits accruing to their institutions from an increased student population than in the needs of the most disadvantaged among the adult population. The material is vast, and new thinking scarce.

"Limits of the Scientific Inquiry." *Daedalus*, Vol. 107, No. 2, Spring 1978.

This issue is the result of a continuing seminar, founded at the Massachusetts Institute of Technology and chaired by Professors Gerald Holton and Robert Morison. Walter Rosenblith, provost of MIT, in a letter that set the tone for the inquiry, pointed out that the agreement scientists and scholars have had with society regarding the production of ideas and devices with minimal restraints is in danger of breaking down or, at least, needs revision. This issue of *Daedalus* is dedicated to dealing with the practical problems now being faced in the scholarly and scientific community. The debate focuses on authority and its relation to political power. Who can decide what boundaries to impose on scientific inquiry? What is good for humanity? How does the scientific community decide what it should do, and when?

Lindner, Eileen W. "Our Classist Army." In *Christianity and Crisis*, Vol. 37, No. 8, May 16, 1977.

A strong statement that volunteers for the Army, like many of

their predecessors who were drafted, come from among the poor
and minorities. Recruiters go where they are most apt to be successful: to the inner-city and rural areas where, rather than face
unemployment, youth seek a secure future.

"Literacy and Population." *Population Bulletin*, Vol. 30, No. 2. Washington, D.C.: Population Reference Bureau, 1975.
     A summary of literacy in relation to family-planning. Illiteracy
is presented as one of the chief obstacles to the dissemination of
family-planning information. The assumption that literacy leads
to development seems to prevail in this approach.

McDermott, R. P. "Achieving School Failure: An Anthropological
Approach to Illiteracy and Social Stratification." *In Education and
Cultural Process*, George D. Spindler, ed. New York: Holt, Rinehart
and Winston, 1974.
     The author contends that the interaction of intelligent, socially
competent children from a low-status or pariah community and
hard-working, intelligent, well-intentioned teachers from a dominant or host community can be as disastrous as the combination
of physically disabled children and socially disabled or prejudiced
teachers. The break-down in communication is inevitable. School
learning is shunned by many otherwise able children because of
this miscommunication. Ethnic, racial, and class boundaries are
too strong to be overcome and school failure becomes a peer-
group status symbol. The high rate of reading disability among
minority children can be explained in terms of cultural conflict.

Minzey, Jack D., and Le Tarte, Clyde. *Community Education: From
Program to Process*. Midland, Mich.: Pendell, 1972.
     A presentation of the rationale for community education as a
means of involving individuals in community action. The authors
discuss the funding and recruitment of adults for education programs and call for local coordination of programs offered.

Monthly Labor Review.
     See *Special Labor Force Reports*.

Morris, Horace W. "They Are a Lost Generation." In *The New York
Times*, Feb. 7, 1977.
     In this article for the *New York Times* Op-Ed page, Horace W.
Morris, the executive director of the New York Urban League,
discusses the situation of minority youths between the ages of 17
and 22, a group he calls "a lost generation." Morris discusses
past programs, most of them federally funded, that failed to solve
the problems of these youngsters. The deprivation they suffer
results from their parents' having been deprived; if these minority
youngsters are not helped, they will pass the same problems on
to their children.

Murphy, Richard T. *Final Report: Adult Functional Reading Study*. Washington, D.C.: National Institute of Education, 1973.

The study conducted by the Educational Testing Service (ETS) began with a national study to determine typical adult reading tasks. An instrument was developed and a national survey was conducted to determine the ability of adults to perform the tasks.

Nafziger, Dean H., et al. *Tests of Functional Adult Literacy: An Evaluation of Currently Available Instruments*. Portland, Ore.: Assessment Projects, Northwest Regional Laboratory, 1975.

A presentation of the problems in measuring functional literacy and a demonstration of the spread of estimates regarding literacy resulting from different instruments. The various tests are evaluated for reliability according to a set of uniform criteria. The study concludes that few instruments have been developed for adults and that much more work needs to be done in the field.

National Advisory Council on Adult Education (NACAE). *Beyond the Verge*. Section I. Washington, D.C.: NACAE, 1977.

A report of the activities of the National Advisory Council in 1976, including an accounting of regional meetings held with adult education practitioners across the country to ascertain their needs and recommendations in anticipation of new legislation to be enacted at the expiration of the Adult Education Act in 1978.

National Advisory Council on Adult Education. *Federal Activities in Support of Adult Education*. Washington, D.C.: NACAE, 1972.

A directory of federal programs that provide adult education in all areas and subjects. Lack of coordination among programs is highlighted and an agency to provide this function is called for. The material is dated, as many programs have disappeared. However, the basic situation continues.

National Advisory Council on Adult Education. *Futures and Amendments: Survey of State Support*. Section 2. Washington, D.C.: NACAE, 1977.

Reports on the suggestions resulting from meetings with adult educators; a survey of publicly funded adult education in 1976, state by state; conclusions and recommendations of the NACAE. The appendix includes state education agency organization charts; examples of state legislation and regulations for adult education; state allotment of federal funds; and the text of the Adult Education Act.

National Advisory Council on Adult Education. *A Target Population in Adult Education*. Washington, D.C.: NACAE, 1974.

This report of the NACAE is an ambitious attempt to bring together statistics describing the educationally disadvantaged and descriptions of some of the effects of educational, economic, and social deprivation. Although much of the statistical material is dated and must be corrected by later reports, no similar attempt of such a comprehensive nature has been made. Some of the assumptions about the results of ABE in enabling participants to find and hold jobs can be questioned. However, the format is clear and the data and comments of the authors are helpful to anyone who wishes to understand the basic facts about the condition of undereducated adults—who they are, where they are, and what they face.

The New York Times. "Illegal Aliens," May 1, 1977.
      This article discusses the confusion caused by available statistics on illegal aliens in the U.S. The U.S. Immigration Service puts the figure at a minimum of 850,000, with other estimates ranging from 2 to 20 million. "Most prudent officials first settle on a figure of around 8 million, then qualify it by saying 'give or take 5 million.' "

The New York Times. "New York Is Lowest in Youth Employment," Aug. 2, 1977.
      This article by Charlayne Hunter-Gault cites a recent federal report stating that New York City has the highest rate of youth unemployment among 11 major American cities. As of June 1977, 74 percent of New York City whites between the ages of 16 and 19 and 86 percent of blacks and other minorities did not have a full-time job. National rates were 42.1 percent for whites and 66.3 percent for minorities.

Olson, David, R. "A Review of *Toward a Literate Society*, edited by Carroll and Chall." Reprinted from *Proceedings of the National Academy of Education*. Vol. 2, 1975.
      The review deals not so much with the content of the volume itself as with the writer's convictions that the original objectives of the Right to Read program are unattainable. He discusses the "literacy myth," i.e., a mistaken faith in the power of literacy to eliminate the social and personal consequences of a myriad of unrelated deprivations. He addresses the consequences of literacy from an historical and cultural perspective, pointing out the effects on mental skills of the primacy of written texts in Western cultures. He concludes by calling the original Right to Read program "a promise to do the impossible" and advocates settling for some basic research, modest gains, and pilot literacy programs.

Osso, Nicolas A. *Adult Basic and Secondary Level Program Statistics*. Washington, D.C.: National Center for Educational Statistics, 1975.
      A study of participation in ABE that also presents data on dropouts. At least one-third of enrollees dropped out annually between 1968 and 1970. Many give their job situation as their

reason, but a larger proportion cites lack of interest. The author notes that about 15 percent who began finished eighth grade.

Participation in Adult Education: Final Report 1972. From an original draft prepared by Imogene E. Okes, Adult and Vocational Education Surveys Branch. Washington, D.C.: National Center for Educational Statistics, 1976.

A statistical survey, based on the Adult Education Supplement to the May 1972 *Current Population Survey*, of persons enrolled in adult education programs during the year ending May 1972. The report shows a 21 percent increase in participation over three years, to a total number of participants of almost 16 million, among whom, however, only 4 percent had not completed high school. Includes charts and some 50 tables analyzing kinds of courses taken, dropout rates, participation rates by level of educational attainment, age, sex, race, family income, etc. Confirms that participants in adult education tend to come from higher-income families. Appendix includes survey instruments and selected questions from Census Bureau's interview card pertinent to participation in adult education.

Participation in Adult Education 1975. Washington, D.C.: National Center for Educational Statistics, forthcoming.

Updated information in the same format as previous entry.

Patten, T. H., and Clark, C. E., Jr. "Literacy Training of Hard-Core Unemployed Negroes in Detroit." In *Journal of Human Resources*, Vol. 2, 1968, pp. 25–36.

The study raises questions about the assumption that improved literacy leads to greater employment opportunities. The subjects in this research did not attribute job attainment to newly acquired reading skills.

Persell, Caroline Hodges. *Education and Inequality*. New York: The Free Press, 1977.

The author analyzes current educational research and sets forth the thesis that a less-favored position in the structure of dominance—whether dominance is based on wealth, market-position, or caste—will be related to lower educational achievements in all societies (including our own) whose educational system is called upon to legitimize social inequities. She further states that in "capitalized" industrialist societies, position in the class structure is the most important correlate of educational attainment. She suggests that the way to rectify such inequalities is to reduce the inequalities in the larger society, and to eliminate or minimize tracking procedures in the schools or having them occur as late in one's educational career as possible—based on justifiable criteria, that is, related to objective predictions of future behaviors and competencies.

Piven, Frances Fox, and Cloward, Richard A. *Regulating the Poor: The Functions of Public Welfare*. New York: Vintage Books, Random House, 1972.

A radical examination of the function of welfare in providing incentives for the poor to accept demeaning labor at low wages rather than suffer degrading and punitive treatment as welfare recipients. The authors survey the history of the expansion and contraction of welfare programs in recent years, pointing to their use as a means of quieting social unrest. They focus on the welfare rights movements of the 1960s and conclude that an aroused poor can sometimes get a response—not to their need, but to the trouble they make. They examine, as well, the results of increased political power for the urban poor and its upsetting impact on local, entrenched power in schools, neighborhoods, jobs, and public services. They also note that greatly increased "advocacy services" of the 1960s have led to many more persons on the welfare rolls.

Postman, Neil. "Illiteracy in America—Position Papers: The Politics of Reading." In *Harvard Educational Review*, Vol. 40, No. 2., May 1970.

Dr. Postman challenges the common assumptions that attaining literacy is politically neutral and is the only, or even the best, avenue to jobs and aesthetic riches. He sees a predominantly literacy-based curriculum as reactionary in the context of recent advances in electronic communications technology and recommends broadening the base of school curricula to include "multimedia literacy."

He contends that schools do not deal with the areas of life in which most problems arise: mental health, sex, and family problems. He raises, also, serious questions about the influence of the printed word as the keystone of education, pointing out its tendency to foster political and social stasis.

Report of the North Carolina Conference to the Division of Adult Education Programs. Washington, D.C.: U.S. Office of Education, 1970.

Earliest thinking of experts that later gave impetus to the APL project.

Resnick, Daniel P., and Resnick, Lauren B. "The Nature of Literacy: An Historical Exploration." In *Harvard Educational Review*, Vol. 47, No. 3, August 1977.

A historical perspective on the present debate over reading achievement. The authors conclude that reading instruction has been aimed at attaining either a low level of literacy for a large number of people or a high level of literacy for an elite. Thus, the present expectation of high levels of literacy for the entire population represents a very recent development.

"Revolting Development: An Exchange with Ivan Illich." In *World Education REPORTS*, No. 14. New York: World Education, 1977.
Edited from a taped transcript of an address by Illich before the Society for International Development, in which he attacks development professionals as need-definers and problem-perceivers.

Rosenthal, Edward Lee. *Politics and Lifelong Learning: An Exploration of Citizen Strategies*. New Brunswick, N.J.: Rutgers Labor Education Center, 1976.
Advocates the establishment of community Learning Opportunities Councils. The paper presents the case for such councils to serve as the means for encouraging learning by all citizens through articulation of needs and opportunities, coordination, publicity, consumer advocacy, and information collection and dissemination.

Rosenthal, Edgar Lee. "Testimony Regarding Lifetime Learning Act." In *Lifetime Learning Act, 1975*. Hearing Before the Committee on Labor and Public Welfare. U.S. Senate, 94th Cong., Dec. 18, 1975.
A call for more adequate distribution of educational services to working-class and poor adults.

Roszak, Theodore. *Where the Wasteland Ends*. New York: Doubleday and Co., 1973.
The author maintains that the technological industrial society is based only on the scientific way of knowing. He decries the artificial environment created by the scientific age, with its arid style of politics and its narrow area of consciousness. He makes the case for mystical, imaginative, symbolic, experimental ways of knowing and a dedication to the discovery of the inner rhythm of creation and eternity.

Roy, Prodipto, and Kapoor, J. M. *The Retention of Literacy*. Delhi: Macmillan Company of India, Ltd., 1975.
The book contains a description of the first systematic study done in India of literacy retention. Its conclusion is that the government should make literacy compulsory through the fifth grade, which they find is the minimal level necessary to guarantee relatively high levels of retention. They recommend also some cohesive follow-up programs.

Rubin, Lillian Breslow. *Worlds of Pain*. New York: Basic Books, 1976.
This book is based on interviews that Rubin, a sociologist, had with working-class American families. In these conversations Rubin discovered that working-class Americans, while better off

financially than those below the poverty level, are subject to many of the same frustrations as the more obviously disadvantaged. In school they become victims of a tracking system that often makes them ineligible for higher education; many lack information about sex and contraception, and so marry and become parents while too young to cope fully with adult responsibilities. Working-class women—whose education restricts them to "girls' subjects," such as home economics and clerical work, thereby denying them access to skilled trades and unionized fields—suffer most from the lack of options. Moreover, parents whose lives have been educationally, emotionally, and financially pinched will rear their children as they themselves were reared. *Worlds of Pain* is valuable because it studies a group of Americans whose problems are often neglected.

Saxe, Natalie, and deLone, Richard H. "Political Implications of a National Reading Effort," in *Toward a Literate Society*, Carroll, John B., and Chall, Jeanne, eds. New York: McGraw-Hill, Inc., 1975.
    The authors address the problem of political action on behalf of illiterate adults, a powerless, unorganized constituency. They point out that the business of remedying injustices is not popular— especially in periods of economic recession.

Schumacher, E. F. *Small Is Beautiful: Economics as if People Mattered*. New York: Harper and Row, 1973.
    An economist examines his own "science," calling into question the presuppositions of his colleagues and their contribution to the conventional theories on which industrial societies rest. The author, an ardent supporter of Gandhi and of Third World approaches to development, rejects "bigness" and Western models. He calls for a return to humanist social wisdom and moral principles as the basis for planning the world's future. In answer to the question, "What can I do?" he replies, "Work to put our own house in order."

Scribner, Sylvia, and Cole, Michael. *Literacy Without Schooling: Testing for Intellectual Effects*. Vai Literacy Project, Working Paper No. 2, New York: Rockefeller University, April 1978.
    In this working paper the authors reflect on the findings of the Vai Literacy Project in the context of the psychology of literacy. They draw tentative conclusions from the Vai study for literacy practice elsewhere—including the fact that certain cognitive skills show little applicability to a broad range of other tasks. Highly organized technical skills like literacy are applied to wider ranges of tasks in complex societies. Research could profitably be directed to the separate analysis of various activities connected with literacy. What do people in various walks of life actually do with literacy? They suggest that reading and writing activities need to be tailored to desired outcomes defined in terms of literacy skills

that enable the individual to continue to master more demanding reading and writing tasks *after* any program is concluded.

Seifer, Nancy. *Absent From the Majority: Working-Class Women in America*. New York: The American Jewish Committee, 1973.
This is a report on a national project on ethnic America—a depolarization program of the American Jewish Committee. The author points out that far less is known about working-class women than about either middle-class or poorer women. She describes the reactions of white ethnic women and their families to changes in the society that threaten their life-style and cites statistics to indicate their unique situation regarding work, family, education, and community expectations. Her analysis is that working-class women can, and probably will, provide a strong, humanizing influence in political life, the labor movement, and in their communities as they find advocates, gain skills to organize, and speak out on issues that affect not only their own lives but those of many others. The study concludes with a set of recommendations.

Sennett, Richard, and Jonathan Cobb. *The Hidden Injuries of Class*. New York: Alfred A. Knopf, Inc., 1972.
This book describes how people perceive education, income, and the type of work they do as worthwhile or not, and why many blue-collar workers, though well-paid, continue to feel, and are often made to feel, beyond the pale of "culture," "taste," or "dignity."

Sheehan, Susan. *A Welfare Mother*. Boston: Houghton-Mifflin, 1976.
In *A Welfare Mother*, originally published as a *New Yorker* profile, Susan Sheehan focuses on Carman Santana (a pseudonym), a welfare mother living in Brooklyn with her common-law husband and the four youngest of her nine children. Sheehan's account of Mrs. Santana's life shows how the cycle of poverty is perpetuated from generation to generation, especially among poor women. Like her mother, Mrs. Santana married and became pregnant while still in her teens, as have her older daughters. Sheehan also makes clear that Mrs. Santana remains on welfare not so much because she is unwilling to work, as because she has no access to information, no knowledge of her options. "Mrs. Santana thinks she will probably go back to work when Maria is grown. She has no idea what jobs there may be in New York City that will pay a living wage to a middle-aged Puerto Rican woman with an eighth grade education who speaks so-so English, possesses no skills, and suffers from bronchitis." Sheehan records the details of the Santanas' lives without making value judgments, and by doing so gives the reader an unusually vivid picture of urban poverty in America.

Sheffield, James. *Retention of Literacy and Basic Skills*. New York: World Bank, 1977.

A review of the literature on retention of literacy and basic cognitive skills. The author concludes that there is no known threshold of educational level for permanent literacy. Many variables—family background, social milieu, and other personal factors—affect retention. There is some indication that adults in short and/or intensive courses do better than those in long ones, but studies of retention present results that are generally contradictory and inconclusive.

Soedjamoko. "Technology, Development, and Culture: A Memorandum for Discussion," in *Education and Development Reconsidered*, The Bellagio Conference Papers. New York: Praeger, 1974.

A strong call from an Indonesian thinker for a world civilization that will be less wasteful of the planet's resources and will place moral values at the center of decision-making. He stresses the interdependence of all peoples in a common future.

Special Labor Force Reports. Washington, D.C.: U.S. Bureau of Labor Statistics, 1969–1977.

The U.S. Bureau of Labor Statistics issues a *Monthly Labor Review*, which provides a useful source of data and analysis. Reprints of *Special Labor Reports* that have been published in the *Monthly Labor Review* are available. A partial listing of those pertinent to a study of the educationally disadvantaged suggests the range of data available. No. 118: The Long-Duration Unemployed; no.'s 121, 131, 145 and 155: Employment of High School Graduates and Dropouts; no. 122: Education of Adult Workers: Projections to 1985; no.'s 125, 140, and 148: Educational Attainment of Workers, March 1969, 1970, 1971 and 1972; no.'s 129 and 143: Employment and Unemployment in 1970, 1971; no. 157: Job Losers, Leavers and Entrants: Traits and Trends.

Srinivasan, Lyra. "The Changing Situation—ABE and the World." Address delivered at the Consultation on Literacy/Adult Basic Education in the 1980s, sponsored by Intermedia at Stony Point, New York, March 1977.

The author traces changing world conditions and attitudes toward development, including its personal aspects as it affects individual lives. She sees the educator's role as that of alleviating human suffering. She discusses conceptual frameworks for seeing the educator's role in development. Three approaches for basic education are outlined: performance-oriented; increasing the power imbalance by attempting to overcome feelings of powerlessness and voicelessness in the learners; and developing the learner's underutilized potential of creativity. This places priority on the third approach as more comprehensive and productive in the light of contemporary demands on individuals to change basic behavior rather than merely to adapt.

Srinivasan, Lyra. *Perspectives in Nonformal Adult Learning*. New York: World Education, 1977.

The author describes the field of nonformal adult education as still evolving and open. She mentions recent influences on nonformal education from the thinking of Illich and Freire, Rogers and Maslow, Skinner, Bruner, and Knowles. One of the major strengths of the monograph is the inclusion of illustrative models of different approaches (gathered from the author's personal experience and from World Education's work) in Thailand, Ethiopia, the Philippines, Bangladesh, Ghana, and other places, including the U.S. She offers sample exercises and activities used in adult education practice and points to specific implications for teacher/leader—training growing out of two approaches: problem-centered and self-actualizing education.

Stauffer, John. *The NALA Study*. A Description of the National Affiliation for Literacy Advance (NALA). Syracuse, N.Y.: New Readers Press, 1973.

A study of tutors and learners in the U.S. Laubach Literacy System detailing the educational background, age, race, and sex of participants.

Sticht, T. G.; Caylor, J. S.; Kern, R. P.; and Fox, L. C. "Project REALISTIC: Determination of Adult Functional Literacy Levels." *Reading Research Quarterly*. Vol. 7, 1972, pp. 424–465.

The research team attempted to discover whether scores on standardized tests of reading achievement were good predictors of job performance. "Readability" estimates were made of written materials in the repairman's, supply clerk's, and cook's jobs. It was discovered that the readability estimate exceeded the reading levels of low-aptitude men by six to eight grade levels.

Sticht, T. G., et al. *HumRRO's Literacy Research for the U.S. Army: Progress and Prospects*. Alexandria, Va.: HumRRO's Professional Paper 2-73, January 1973.

Sticht et al. conclude from studying the results of literacy training in the Army, Navy, and Air Force (including their own program) that the results will be short-lived because they fail to achieve the reading levels needed for even the least-demanding jobs and because job training programs attended after the basic literacy courses made no attempt to build on the literacy training by supplying easy reading materials related to the job.

Sticht, T. G., ed. *Reading for Working: A Functional Literacy Anthology*. Alexandria, Va.: Human Resources Research Organization, 1975.

Discusses research to develop general methods for estimating functional literacy demands of jobs. Suggests methods of reducing discrepancies between personal literacy skills and the literacy demands of the job.

Theobald, Robert. *Beyond Despair*. Washington, D.C.: New Republic Book Company, 1976.
A provocative treatment of the "end of the industrial era" theme. Description of a model for citizen discussion and action around such issues as education, health, justice, and work. Includes sections on strategies for creating change and movement toward a more human environment through greater participation of persons at all social levels in defining the future they desire.

Thompson, Marguerite. *Developing a Positive Self-Image in the Inner City Minority Child Through the Use of the Community as a Classroom/Weeksville*. Ph.D. dissertation. Walden School of Advanced Studies, University of Rhode Island, 1976.
Describes the effect of the archaeological dig in Weeksville (Brooklyn, New York) on children at P.S. 243, and the resulting sense of pride in their own history. One section deals with the effects on the children's parents.

Weber, Rose-Marie. "Adult Illiteracy in the U.S." In *Toward a Literate Society*, Carroll, John B., and Chall, Jeanne, eds. New York: McGraw-Hill, Inc., 1975.
A comprehensive treatment of adult illiteracy within the boundaries of a traditional approach to the concept of literacy. It is lively, interesting, and thorough; the best summary of its kind that we found. It makes an excellent starting point for everyone who is beginning to search for facts in this field.

Weintraub, Bernard. "Navy Recruiting Is Hampered by Illiteracy," in *The New York Times*, Dec. 8, 1977.
According to this *New York Times* article, illiteracy is a serious problem among potential U.S. Navy recruits, with Detroit the most severely affected: nine out of ten youths seeking to enlist are rejected by that district office because they cannot read well enough to pass the Armed Forces Vocational Aptitude Battery.
The Navy has begun a 4 to 6 week pilot program for youths who read below sixth grade level; those who are unable to function beyond sixth grade level after having completed the course are discharged.

Wirtz, Willard, and the National Manpower Institute. *The Boundless Resource*. A Prospectus for an Education-Work Policy. Washington, D.C.: New Republic Book Company, Inc., 1975.

A call for the realigning of established institutional sovereignties to develop new policy and practice in education and work. One central emphasis in the recommendations is that a process be developed at the community level to draw on the American citizen's desire to participate more fully in "the improvement of the human prospect" through the establishment of citizen councils to plan for more rational [and effective] structures of work and education.

Young, Anne M. "Going Back to School at 35." In *Monthly Labor Review*, October 1973. Washington, D.C.: U.S. Department of Labor, Bureau of Labor Statistics.
   A report on a study by the Department of Labor showing that of students aged 35 and older, three-fourths are in the labor force. About 100,000 working persons over 35 were in elementary or secondary school.

Ziegler, Warren L. "On Civic Literacy." An unpublished draft paper. Syracuse, N.Y.: Educational Policy Research Center, 1974.
   The author sees civic literacy as an antidote to dissatisfaction with a depersonalized society. It represents a proactive stance that endeavors to change conditions, not adapt to them. He analyzes the prevailing situation in which there is no public policy that encourages citizens to develop the skills and understanding necessary to engage with politics and with nonpolitical structure. He calls on adult educators to address this area of need and to help adult learners learn the language of political intentions and action.

Ziegler, Warren L. "Who Benefits from Illiteracy? A Radical Critique of the Client Society." Presented at a Symposium on Adult Functional Literacy, 104th Annual Forum, National Conference on Social Welfare, 1977.
   Ziegler states that illiteracy is symptomatic of an underlying problem in American society: the impotence of persons in all walks of life to affect their lives in a meaningful way, their inability to act in their own behalf. He claims that dependency has become an accepted state in a "client society," and illustrates his point from the field of health care, saying that Americans have been made to feel incompetent (illiterate) in the area of their own health needs, so specialized has medical practice become. He also asserts that no economist or statistician knows how many Americans would seek employment if factors depriving them of opportunity were removed. He observes that if illiterate persons intend to aquire conventional competence in reading and writing, it is because that action will have consequences both for themselves and others. Finally, he calls for radical social and economic change and describes some of the implications of such change.

2A. DEMONSTRATION PROJECTS, METHODS, AND EVALUATION

Adams, Dewey Allen. *Review and Synthesis of Research Concerning Adult Vocational and Technical Education*. Columbus, Ohio: Ohio State University, 1972.

A review of the literature on the role of public schools and community colleges in providing adult vocational/technical education. The author advocates a diversity of agencies and approaches, which, he believes, will lead to increased communication between service agencies in the future.

Adult Basic Education and Literacy Activities in Canada, 1975–76. A report of a project undertaken for World Literacy of Canada to survey the nature and extent of functional illiteracy in Canada, with a focus on those activities currently being undertaken in English-speaking Canada. By Audrey M. Thomas. World Literacy of Canada, April 1976.

The data are based on school completion figures, grade 9 being the level chosen as constituting functional literacy. In Canada the total population 15 years old and over not attending school (in 1971) was over 13 million and those with less than grade 9 were almost 4 million, or 39 percent of the out-of-school adult population.

Various programs for this population are described without evaluation.

Adult Basic Education Component: Manpower Development Component; and Program Evaluation. Final Report. Greenville, Miss.: Delta Opportunities Corporation, 1972.

Overall description of the program. One recommendation to be noted is: "With some form of transportation allowance, the average daily attendance is much higher."

Adult Basic Education Demonstration Project: Final Evaluation Report. Chattanooga, Tenn.: Chattanooga Public Schools, 1972.

Twenty-nine "process objectives" were used to evaluate a curriculum. Curriculum content divided into three areas: (1) derived—prevocational, typing, clothes construction; (2) generic—reading, handwriting, spelling; and (3) life-style—field trips, arts and crafts.

Adult Basic Education Program. Columbus, Ohio: Columbus Public Schools, 1974.

The ABE program serves 1,900 inner-city adults of all ages and of several ethnic groups. New students are interviewed by a reading counselor who subsequently follows their progress. Persons at a fourth grade reading level or lower work together in small groups in a reading laboratory.

Adult Basic Education Project: Career Centers Program. Division of Extension and Continuing Education, University of Puerto Rico, Final Report. Rio Piedras: University of Puerto Rico, Division of Extension and Continuing Education, 1974.

This was a three-year demonstration project to reduce educational and occupational disadvantages of unemployed and underemployed Puerto Rican adults. The average student attended 24 days once a week and advanced one to three grades. The three main programming areas were staff development, curriculum development, and student participation.

The Adult Basic Education Program: Progress in Reducing Illiteracy and Improvements Needed. General Accounting Office (GAO) Report to Congress. Washington, D.C.: U.S. Office of Education, 1975.

ABE programs in California, Illinois, North Carolina, Texas, and Virginia were reviewed to assess progress made in reducing illiteracy. The report concludes that the program reaches only a fraction of those needing it. It notes a lack of realistic, measurable program goals and evaluative criteria, misdirected recruitment procedures, and a lack of coordination with federal antipoverty programs. Recommendations for combating these and other problems are included.

Adult Reading-Bilingual Laboratories and Learning Center, Huntsville, Texas. Texas State Department of Correction, Huntsville-Windham School District, Texas Criminal Justice Council, 1973.

This program served 1,221 inmates of nine prison units who were released three hours per week from work assignments. Some were Spanish-speaking, others were English-speaking blacks and whites. An individually based approach was used after testing for the highest level at which inmates could read without difficulty. "Methods of teaching reading include language experience approach, commercial programmed materials, a kinesthetic approach and a phonetic approach."

Appalachian Right To Read Community-Based Centers. Morehead, Ky.: Morehead State University, Appalachian Adult Education Center, 1973.

Names of potential students were obtained from the state employment office, which identified persons applying for jobs who lacked a high school degree. The best source of students was other successful students. Reading materials for preschoolers of the adult students were purchased and delivered to home readers.

Arter, Rhetta. *Operation Cope: A Family Learning Center: Evaluation 1975.* Washington, D.C.: National Council of Negro Women, 1975.

Participants in this multiservice center educational program helped plan their learning activities. The target population comprised mothers under age 36 who were heads of households, who scored below eighth grade on standardized tests, and whose incomes were below the poverty level. Educational program content was built around coping skills directed toward employment.

Atkin, J. Myron. "On Looking Gift Horses in the Mouth: The Federal Government and the Schools." In *Educational Forum*, Vol. 34, November 1969.

This article presents the case against federal support of education, based on the government's inability to address long-term problems and its demands for standardization.

Barrio Education Project. *Education, Critical Awareness, Participation*. San Antonio: n.d.

A brief description of programs and approaches to community education and development in the Mexican American community in San Antonio.

Beder, Harold W., III. "Community Linkages in Urban Public School Adult Basic Education Programs: A Study of Co-Sponsorship and the Use of Community Liaison Personnel." Unpublished Ph.D. dissertation, Columbia University, 1972.

A study of ABE programs that worked cooperatively with community agencies. ABE benefits by the help received in enrolling students. Difficulties include the time required to maintain the linkages. The provision of ABE services helps the community agencies fulfill their mandate to serve the community.

Blake, Howard E., and Sackett, Duane H. "Curriculum for Improving Communication Skills: A Language Arts Handbook for Use in Corrections." *A Monograph Series for Correctional Educators, No. 3*. Washington, D.C.: American Bar Association, The Clearing House for Offender Literacy Programs, 1975.

Deals with designing programs for transient students and suggests learning activities to be used in such programs.

Brehmer, Margaret, ed. *AIM: A Creative Approach to Teaching Adults*. New York: World Education, 1977.

A teachers' guide to using and creating learning materials for adults based on their own life experience. The loose-leaf manual, designed as a supplement to other basic education materials, contains a discussion of AIM (Apperception-Interaction Method), a selection of teacher-written, open-ended stories for discussion, and specific instructions for preparing and using such materials.

Brooks, Elva. *Project Open-Out: Adult Basic Education*. Final Report. Washington, D.C.: U.S. Office of Education, 1975.

Includes annotated list of teaching materials found useful in this project. Staff felt that door-to-door canvassing was a more effective recruitment procedure than word-of-mouth.

Burch, Sandra. "Instead of Corner Hustlers: Youth Emulate Police Team." In *The News and Courier, Charleston Evening Post, SUNDAY*. Charleston, S. C.: July 10, 1977.
An account of the "Septima Clark '77" project of the Charleston East Side Police Team's summer program, modeled on Septima Clark's earlier experience with the Southern Christian Leadership Conference Voter Registration Project.

Centers for Community Education Development. Brochure published by C. S. Mott Foundation, Flint, Mich.: 1975.
Contains a directory of Centers for Community Education and Development in 47 states. Centers—often based in universities— are set up to assist citizens to obtain training, resources, and information on how to mobilize for local action. As far as we could discover, the Appalachian Adult Education Center at Morehead State University in Kentucky was the only one dealing specifically with community education and development for disadvantaged adults.

*Clark, Septima. *Echo in My Soul*. New York: E. P. Dutton Co., 1962.
Contains a vivid description of the early efforts of the Southern Christian Leadership Conference to establish voter registration schools using local community leaders as teachers.

Drake, James Bob, and Morgan, Alice S. "A Career Decision-Making Model Utilizing Adult Basic Education and Counseling for the Under/Unemployed Adult and Family." Final Report. Auburn, Ala.: Auburn University, Alabama Department of Vocational and Adult Education, Huntsville City Schools, 1974.
Discusses methods used to recruit ABE students, including a mobile "learning van."

The Educational Programs of Laubach Literacy International. Brochure. Syracuse, N.Y.: Laubach Literacy International, 1976.
The basic approach of the Laubach method is described.

Evaluation of the Community-Based Right-to-Read Program. Berkeley, Calif.: Pacific Training and Technical Assistance Project, 1974.
A study and evaluation of 24 community-based Right to Read projects in California.

Federally Funded Adult Basic Education Programs. New York: Xerox Corporation, 1967.
A survey of the ABE programs in ten states. The report analyzes ABE as a subsystem of the antipoverty program. It concludes that if ABE is to serve the real needs of the illiterate poor, it must move away from a traditional school model and develop more adequate social-action initiatives that would respond to the civic problems of the poor as well as their educational needs. The

survey asserts that ABE does not significantly contribute to employment options for students.

Friedman, Burton D., and Dunbar, Laird J. *Grants Management in Education: Federal Impact on State Agencies*. Chicago: Public Administration Service, 1971.

Decries federal grants practices of the Office of Education as incapable of fostering effectiveness and autonomy on the part of state education agencies.

General Description of Programs and Services. Syracuse, N.Y.: Literacy Volunteers of America, Inc. n.d.

An outline of the resources and training offered by LVA.

"Gila River Indian Community ABE Experimental Demonstration Project: Final Report, June 3, 1972–May 31, 1973." Sacaton, Ariz.: Gila River Indian Community, 1973.

The objective of this program was to provide tutoring in a learning center, in jail, in an alcoholic halfway house and in participants' homes. Local residents were trained to tutor and counsel.

Granger, James C., ed. *Abstracts of Selected Cooperative Adult Education Programs*. Columbus, Ohio: Ohio State University, Center for Vocational Education, 1975.

For each program the author indicates the components supplied by the industry (e.g., facilities, released time, materials) and the components supplied by the affiliated state agency (e.g., planning assistance, texts, facilities). This is a nationwide picture and includes heavy industry, food-processing companies, and service industries.

Greenleigh Associates. *Field Test and Evaluation of Selected Adult Basic Education Systems*. New York: Greenleigh Associates, 1966.

An evaluation of four systems of teaching reading to illiterates (below eighth grade level). The authors assert that teachers with no more than a high school education were more effective than more highly educated teachers.

"A Guide to Using Language Experience with Adults." Cambridge, Mass.: Community Learning Center, 1973.

The emphasis of this program was on communications, providing an atmosphere of sharing and personal growth and allowing students to confront their own learning blocks rather than ignore them. Methods included: dictation, transcription, directed writing, and free writing. Emphasis was on student-created materials.

Hall, Paul R., and others. *Literacy Education Among Adult Indians in Oklahoma*. Vol. 1. Washington, D.C.: U.S. Office of Education, Office of Indian Education, 1977.

A random sample of Native Americans in Oklahoma found at least 16,000 more in that state than had been previously thought. Data are included on educational levels of the Native American population as well as functional literacy levels. Severe functional illiteracy was found in consumer, health, and computational areas.

Volumes 2 and 3 have supporting evidence for the appendixes in Volume 1.

Heart of the Earth Survival School. Minneapolis: Longie Printing Co., 1976.

A brochure describing this school's approach to teaching the history, traditions, and lore of Native Americans.

Interrelating Library and Basic Education Services for Disadvantaged Adults: A Demonstration of Four Alternative Working Models. Annual Report, Vol. 2. Morehead, Ky.: Appalachian Adult Education Center, Morehead State University, 1974.

A theoretical overview developed as background for the AAEC research into cooperative service to disadvantaged adults. Includes sections on the nature of disadvantaged adults; influence of geographic location on needs; goals of educational and library services; historical and sociological analyses; and the appropriate specialization of libraries and public schools in serving the disadvantaged adult.

Kansas City School District. *Special Project for Coordinated Adult Basic Education, 1968–69*. Final Report. Kansas City, 1969.

Provides an example of local coordination of federally funded agencies in the Kansas City area. Savings in program costs, greater access by all agencies to trained personnel, and the ability to provide daytime classes resulted. The report stresses elements to be included in all such cooperative agreements.

Kent, William P. *Adult Basic Education Programs, Students and Results*. TM Report No. 33. Princeton, N.J.: ERIC Clearinghouse on Tests, Measurements and Evaluation, 1974.

Contains composite data of 2,300 ABE students in 200 classes in 90 programs in 15 states. The study was conducted for the National Institute of Education between 1971 and 1973. Of students enrolled in 1971, less than 40 percent were still attending classes in May 1972.

Lusterman, Seymour. "Education for Work." In *The Conference Board RECORD*, Vol. 13, No. 5, May 1976. New York: The Conference Board.

This article summarizes the judgments of corporate executives—principally senior personnel executives—on the extent to which their companies' educational programs deal with subjects and skills that are appropriate to business and the extent, if any, to which they are a result of failures in other parts of the educational system. The findings rest on the experience of 610 firms selected to represent the universe of companies with 500 or more employees, which account for about one-half of all private employment in the U.S.

Mezirow, Jack; Darkenwald, Gordon F.; and Knox, Alan B. *Last Gamble on Education*. Washington, D.C.: Adult Education Association, 1975.

The report of an unusual study of ABE. Using a "grounded theory" methodology, the research team produced the most extensive, original study of ABE that exists and includes the interests and motivations of participants, characteristics of learners and leaders, classroom dynamics, methods, materials, attitudes, and accomplishments. Their suggested reforms grow out of a realistic analysis of the situation.

McClelland, Samuel. *Project Reach* Final Report, Year 2. South Bend, Ind.: Notre Dame University, 1972.

Reports percentages of students who enrolled in ABE program according to their primary and secondary sources of information. Promotional techniques included ads on matchbook covers, radio broadcasts, TV spots in prime time, newspapers, posters, social agencies, and a door-to-door campaign. The largest proportion were reached through the door-to-door campaign and the TV spots. The two major reasons for dropping out of the program were "conflict with work" (29 percent of the drop-outs) and "no particular reason" (25 percent).

Meyer, Rosemary. *Survey of Adult Basic Education Dropouts at the Dr. Martin Luther King, Jr. Education Center*. Kankakee, Ill.: Dr. Martin Luther King Education Center, 1974.

A seven-month survey of drop-outs was conducted through door-to-door interviews, telephone calls, tape recordings and correspondence. Most frequent reasons given for dropping out were family and personal illness, and problems with transportation, and jobs.

The NALA Directory 1975–76. Syracuse, N.Y.: The National Affiliation for Literacy Advance, 1976.

A listing of organizations for the promotion of literacy using the Laubach method. All maintain an affiliation with the parent organization and subscribe to its training and accreditation requirements.

National Urban League in Action. Summary of Urban League Programs. New York: National Urban League, Inc., n.d.

A description of the services and approaches of one agency that practices education in community settings.

Navajo Adult Basic Education: Final Report 1972–1973. Many Farms, Ariz.: Navajo Community College, 1973.

An all-Navajo staff is involved not only in instruction but in social action as well. There is an English-speaking program for Navajo adults with content based on familiar experiences of the participants. Participation in a voter registration campaign greatly increased the number of Navajo voters and resulted in three Navajos being elected to state and local offices. Measures of success include participants now being able to sign welfare checks and less need for interpreters.

Nickse, Ruth S. "The Central New York External High School Diploma Program." In *Phi Delta Kappan*, October 1975.

and

Nickse, Ruth S. *Development of a Performance Assessment System for the Central New York External High School Diploma Program: An Educational Alternative for Adults*. Syracuse, N.Y.: Regional Learning Service of Central New York, 1975.

and

Nickse, Ruth S. *A Report on Adult Learners: A Profile of Fifty Adult Learners*. Syracuse, N.Y.: Syracuse Research Corporation, January 1976.

These three entries describe the development and implementation of the external high school diploma program in the Syracuse area. They provide a clear picture of the way in which assessment procedures evolved, the actual experience of the first graduates, and the reflections of those responsible for this innovative approach.

A Partial Listing of Cooperative Adult Education Programs. Columbus, Ohio: The Center for Vocational Education, Ohio State University, June 1975.

One of five monographs published as part of a study sponsored by the U.S. Office of Education. The total study is the most comprehensive overview that exists on ABE programs in industry. Together with the Lusterman study, the monographs are essential reading in the area of industry and basic education.

Other monographs include: *Case Studies of Selected Cooperative Adult Education Programs*, *Abstracts of Selected Cooperative Adult Education Programs*, *Discussion of Industry-Education Cooperation for Adult Learning*, and *Guidelines for the Development and Study of Cooperative Adult Education Programs*.

The common introduction to each volume takes issue with the easy promises that improved education will guarantee employment or a better job. The authors point to the importance of stating *specific* objectives for basic education programs, because the variables other than education—economic conditions, motivation, union contracts, and number of jobs available—are more powerful in determining the individual's economic situation than education. The study makes a case for the benefits that accrue both to industry and to state education agencies as a result of cooperative programs, but warns against seeing them as a panacea.

The Plantation Adult Basic Education Program. Abbeville, La.: Southern Mutual Help Association, 1973.

Began as an antipoverty program for sugar cane workers. Program objectives: (1) raising educational level of workers; (2) advising workers of available assistance; (3) assisting workers and their families with diet and food preparation; and (4) teaching budgeting and effective purchasing. Project demonstrated results of integrated approaches to learner needs.

Policies and Procedures Handbook. Syracuse, N.Y.: Literacy Volunteers of America, Inc., 1975.

The requirements and procedures for setting up a local LVA affiliate.

Ryan, T. A., and Furlong, William. "Literacy Programs in Industry, the Armed Forces, and Penal Institutions." In *Toward a Literate Society*, Carroll, John B., and Chall, Jeanne, eds. New York: McGraw-Hill, Inc., 1975.

The authors discuss, in fairly general terms, programs in industry and penal institutions. They report on research related to literacy campaigns in the Army that concluded that these have little effect for a variety for reasons, including lack of coordination with other job-skills programs.

Silvester, John. "A Review of the Status of Supportive Services in Adult Basic Education." Human Renewal Services Demonstration Project (H-085) Interim Report. Godfrey, Ill.: Lewis and Clark Community College, 1976.

Examines the concept of supportive services (counseling, for example) and provides an overview of the current types of supportive services, which include recruitment, retention, and follow-up activities. Report includes a selective bibliography. Lists and discusses methods of recruitment and has three case studies of exemplary programs.

Sjogren, Douglas, and Jacobsen, Larry. *Effective ABE Programs: Nine Case Studies.* Ft. Collins: Colorado State University, 1976.

Describes the contents of urban and rural ABE programs in nine Western locations.

Society for the Preservation of Weeksville and Bedford-Stuyvesant History. Brochure prepared by the Weeksville Society, Brooklyn, N.Y.

A description of an entire community's involvement in the recovery of its history. An archeological dig covering a city block in the present Bedford-Stuyvesant section of Brooklyn yields artifacts that enable present inhabitants of the area to develop curiosity and pride in their past as well as new dedication to building their present community.

Survival School System. St. Paul: American Indian Movement, 1974.
Information brochure on the Survival School approach to the supplementary education of Native Americans of all ages.

VAST [Vocational Adult Secondary Training] Development Project. Phase 1, Final Report. Victoria, B.C.: British Columbia Department of Education, Ottawa, Department of Manpower and Immigration, 1973.
This is a four-part report of a project to develop and revise ABE curricula, building in the concepts of individualized instruction and life-skills training. In a comparison test VAST classes progressed faster than regular classes. Report includes student and instructor manuals, sample units, and a list of commercial materials.

Viznor, Gerald. *Opportunities Unlimited: Minnesota Indians Adult Basic Education*. Narrative and Statistical Evaluation, Third Year, 1971–72, with Review of First Two Years. St. Paul: Minnesota State Department of Education, Indian Section, 1972.
According to attendance records the most popular courses were in beadwork and the Anishabe language, followed by driver training and ABE. Many students who first attended Native American cultures classes subsequently enrolled in other subjects. There were problems of providing childcare for students of ABE and driver education classes.

2B. TEACHERS/PARAPROFESSIONALS

Adult Basic Education National Teacher Training Study: Part III, Survey of Needs. Kansas City: University of Missouri Center for Resource Development in Adult Education, 1972.
A large-scale survey of ABE/GED students, teachers, and administrators showed, among other things, that all the groups tended to prefer traditional patterns of class organization and instructional materials. Students want to be grouped by interest, while teachers and administrators prefer grouping by level. Teachers think specially trained, full-time ABE/GED teachers are most successful; administrators think elementary teachers are most successful.

309b Adult Education Act Replication Guide. Butte, Mont.: Butte Vocational-Technical Center, 1973.

Discusses recruitment, training of aides, programs geared to parents of preschoolers, and teaching students in their homes. Includes a list of commercial materials the staff found useful.

"Adult Education Staff Development Bibliography, U.S. Office of Education Region 3." College Park: University of Maryland, Conference and Institutes Division, 1973.

Includes bibliographies, a list of volunteer associations, and selected adult education journals.

Boggs, David. *Adult Basic Education Teacher Training in Measurement and Diagnosis of Learning and Teaching Reading and Math.* Final Report. Columbus: Ohio State University, 1975.

Describes a workshop in ABE using the TV series *Basic Education: Teaching the Adult,* developed by the University of Maryland. Appears to be a student-centered, individual-focused training experience.

Boggs, David. *A Study of Teacher Aides in Ohio Adult Basic Education Programs.* Columbus: Ohio State Department of Education, 1976.

Offers demographic data on backgrounds of currently employed aides. Examines their preparation for the job and discusses the nature and quality of the working relationship between teachers and aides.

Colorado State University American Indian Adult Basic Education and Administrator Training Project. Terminal Report, 6/30/71—12/31/72. Ft. Collins: Colorado State University, Department of Education, 1972.

This workshop trained people already working or interested in working on reservations. Originally intended to be for Native Americans only, the shortage of Native American participants provided space for other ABE teachers interested in working with Native Americans.

"Demonstration, Developmental and Research Project for Programs, Materials, Facilities and Educational Technology for Undereducated Adults: Ohio State Module. Utilization of Paraprofessionals in Rural ABE programs." Final Report. Morehead, Ky.: Morehead State University, 1971.

The program was designed to serve rural Appalachian whites. Over 300 students were served by eight ABE centers and three home-instruction units. Contains explanations of the procedures and activities used to recruit and train paraprofessionals.

Dowling, William, ed. *Project to Train Adult Basic Education Teachers in Personalized Instruction.* Columbus: Ohio State University, 1974.

Report of a workshop on personalized instruction. Includes

seven papers: Planning for Adult Education; Individualization—
The Release of Human Potential, Using Readability Formulas and
Written Materials for Appropriate Grade Levels; Motivation and
Life Style of ABE Participants; The Role of the Teacher in the
Adult Basic Education Learning Laboratory; Force Field Anal-
ysis; and Non-Verbal Communications in Adult Basic Education.

*Felt Needs for Training by Adult Basic Education Administrators and
Teachers in Texas*. College Station: Texas A&M University, 1972.
　　Ranks topics in which over 30 directors and 200 teachers of
ABE felt they needed additional training. Top two for administrators were recruitment and selecting appropriate instructional
materials. Top two for teachers were discovering needs of students
and selecting appropriate instructional materials.

Martin, McKinley C. "The Association Between In-Service Training
and Teachers' Perception of Selected Program Elements in Adult Basic
Education." Unpublished Ph.D. dissertation, Florida State University,
1972.
　　The writer suggests that in-service training correlates with increased use of instructional aids but has little relation to other
areas of performance.

McGee, Lee, comp. *Selected Strategies for Teaching Adults*. Nashville:
Tennessee State Department of Education, Tennessee State University,
1977.
　　A collection of papers based on presentations by teacher-trainers at an ABE workshop. Notable chapters include those on teaching Indochinese students and teaching study skills.

Mocker, Donald, et al. *Adult Basic Education Teacher Competency
Inventory*. Kansas City: University of Missouri, Center for Resource
Development in Adult Education, 1974.
　　The Adult Basic Education (ABE) teacher inventory is presented in two parts and is intended to determine (1) the respondent's concept of desirable ABE teacher qualifications, and
(2) the respondent's self-assessment of personal ABE teacher
competencies.

Park, Rosemarie J. "Training Teachers in the Area of Adult Literacy:
A Case Study Approach." A paper presented at the Association for
the Development of Computer-Based Instructional Systems, Summer
Conference, Minneapolis, August 1976.
　　Participants in three teacher-training programs tested their skills
in diagnosing problems and prescribing teaching techniques to
solve those problems through the use of computerized case sim-
ulations. Case studies sensitized teachers to the learning problems
of certain populations, familiarized teachers with existing materials, and suggested techniques for developing additional materials.

Project to Teach Educationally Disadvantaged Parents ABE Skills in Their Own Homes and to Show These Parents How and What to Teach Their Pre-School Children. Butte, Mont.: Butte Vocational-Technical Center, 1973.

Preference in the selection of teachers and teacher aides was given to Model Cities residents with preschool experience. Most parents expressed the wish to have more information about creative play, prereading skills, and parent-child activities.

A Replication Handbook for Learning Disabilities and the Institutionalized Adult. A 309 Project for Staff Development of Adult Basic Education Personnel in Iowa. Fayette: Upper Iowa University, n.d.

Contains descriptions of training workshop for teachers of ABE/GED with specific activity suggestions for working with learning-disabled adults.

Teacher Training Institute: Adult Basic Education, July 19–August 6, 1971 and Follow-Up Study, 1972. Montgomery: Alabama State University, 1972.

One hundred participants—administrators and teachers—from 16 states focused on the problems of the rural poor.

Teacher Training Institute Final Project Report. Monmouth, Ore.: Oregon College of Education, 1972.

Report of a summer institute attended by ABE teachers. One-half of the participants were Anglo and the rest were Eskimo or Native American. Long distances and transportation problems inhibit participation in ABE programs. Teachers in rural areas should be prepared for sporadic attendance.

Urban Adult Basic Education Special Teacher Training Institute. Final Report. Los Angeles: Pepperdine University, Center for Urban Affairs, 1972.

Participants were divided into core groups of 15, each under an experienced facilitator. They looked at group process, engaged in field experiences, did individual research projects in local libraries on black and urban problems, and attended lectures.

Volunteer and Adult Basic Reading Tutorial Program. Final Special Demonstration Project Report. Syracuse, N.Y.: Literacy Volunteers, Inc., 1974.

Presents Adult Basic Reading Program offered by Literacy Volunteers of America in eight sites in Connecticut, seven in Massachusetts, and one in New York. Correctional institute inmates served as tutors. Libraries, businesses, and industrial firms were involved in the program. The 18-hour LVA Tutor Training Workshop was refined and improved. Two guides and a diagnostic reading test were developed.

Zinn, Lorraine, M. *Adult Basic Education: Literature Abstracts in Staff Development, 1965–1975*. Kansas City: University of Missouri, Center for Resource Development in Adult Education, 1975.
    Contains 404 abstracts relating to adult education staff development. Each abstract includes the author(s), source and ED (ERIC Document) number.

Zinn, Lorraine. *Adult Basic Education Teacher Competency Inventory*. Kansas City: University of Missouri Center for Resource Development in Adult Education, 1974.
    Thirty-seven of Iowa's 370 ABE teachers used Donald Mocker's 291-item Teacher Competency Inventory to determine the most-needed competencies for Iowa ABE teachers and gave priority to knowledge and behavior about the Iowa learner, curriculum, and instruction.

Zinn, Lorraine. *Adult Basic Education Teacher Competency Inventory: Puerto Rican Final Report*. Kansas City: University of Missouri, 1974.
    Ten percent of Puerto Rican ABE teachers were given an inventory to identify, classify, and rank knowledge, behavior, and attitudes appropriate for ABE teachers. Recommendations include frequent in-service programs, further teaching evaluations, improvement of teacher-training programs, and better communication.

2C. RECRUITMENT AND RETENTION

Many states have developed handbooks and guidelines for recruitment to ABE programs. Teacher-training workshops often include a presentation on recruitment strategies. The following publications are among those which have been developed for this purpose.

Adult Armchair Education Program. *Recruitment Workbooks*. A Branch of the OIC, Inc., 1404 Ridge Ave., Philadelphia, Ronald Howard, Manager.

Appalachian Adult Education Center, Huntsville, Ala. *Training and Use of Volunteer Recruiters in ABE Programs*. June 1971.

Axford, Roger W. *Adult Education: The Open Door*. Scranton, Pa.: International Textbook Co., 1969.

Iowa State Department of Public Instruction. *A Handbook for Recruiting: Adult Basic Education: Iowa*. Des Moines, Iowa, 1974.

Pike, Vicki. *3 R's: Recruitment–Retention–Reward*. Statesboro, Ga.: Georgia Southern College, Adult Education Unit, 1973.

Seaman, Don F. *Preventing Dropouts in ABE*. Tallahassee: Florida State University Adult Education Research Information Processing Center, 1971.

Snyder, Robert. *Recruitment in Adult Basic Education*. Tallahassee: Florida State University, 1971.

Walden, Bobbie. *Recruitment and Retention of Adult Learners*. Montgomery: Alabama State Department of Education, 1975.

2D. CURRICULUM MATERIALS COMMONLY USED

Adult Basic Education: An Evaluation of Materials. Southwestern Cooperative Educational Laboratory, Albuquerque, N.M. Volume 1 contains resource materials on English and English as a Second Language. Volume 2 contains materials on reading, math, citizenship, consumer education, science, health, and social studies. Volume 3 contains resource materials on supplemental language arts, vocational education, social living, General Equivalency Diploma, and English.
　　Each volume has charts of how the material was evaluated, but does not show the material itself.

Adult Basic Education: New Mexico Personal Growth Curriculum. Revised. New Mexico State Department of Education, 1975.
　　Subject areas include family life, health education, the world of work, money management, and citizenship and government. Vocabulary list and/or bibliography is included for most units. Suggests activities with fairly detailed plans for each topic.

AIM [Apperception-Interaction Method]: An Exemplary Program from International Experience. Final Report. New York: World Education, 1975.
　　Application of a modified Freire method in the United States. Contains 101 photo-discussion units and 69 stories.

Applications of the Individually Prescribed Instructional System to ABE Programs in Nevada, June '69 - June '70. Final Project Report. Carson City: Nevada State Department of Education, 1970.
　　Page samples of typical mathematics and reading materials developed in the project are displayed in the index.

Beder, Harold, and Darkenwald, Gordon. *Development, Demonstration and Dissemination: Case Studies of Selected Specific Projects in ABE*. Occasional Paper #42. Syracuse, N.Y.: Publication Program in Continuing Education, Syracuse University, 1974.
　　Includes TV, radio, written materials, and videotapes among its descriptions of the programs.

Ford, Claudette. *Training Workshop for Adult Education Personnel in Cultural and Ethnic Understanding*. Final Report. Washington, D.C.: BLK Group, Inc., 1976.

A *Cultural Awareness Handbook* was developed for teacher-training. The first edition focuses on cultural awareness in general, while the second edition is specifically geared to curriculum development and ethnic bias in teaching materials.

GIFT (Good Ideas for Teaching) Reading. Tuscaloosa: Alabama University, 1972.

This handbook provides guidelines, procedures, and techniques for teaching basic reading to adults. The chapters outline the scope and sequence of an adult basic education course, characteristics of the adult learner, terminology, an ABE assessment instrument, vocabulary, comprehension, study skills, materials, and a bibliography.

Job Application Learning Packet No. 1. Washington, D.C.: American Bar Association, Clearinghouse for Offender Literacy Programs, 1975.

This package of instructional materials is designed to aid adults in prison to learn how to apply for a job. A teacher's guide outlines 14 hours of instruction. Other materials consist of vocabulary flash cards, a student's work sheet, discussion ideas and activities, a sample job application, and brochures on how to get a job. Makes use of many government publications.

Johnson, Charles Ray. *A Curriculum Guide for Mid-Alabama Adult and Vocational Education Demonstration Center*. Tuskegee, Ala.: Tuskegee Institute, 1972.

A listing of curriculum ideas to raise the competencies of adults in several basic areas and on three different levels.

Johnson, Robert. *English as a Second Language for Job Training and Employment: Special Demonstration Project*. San Diego, Calif: San Diego Community College, Division of Adult Education, 1972.

Provides English as a Second Language material aimed at preparing students for job training, on-the-job training, or entry-level employment, mainly in semiskilled occupations.

Kennedy, Katherine, and Roeder, Stephanie. *A Guide to Using Language Experience with Adults*. Cambridge, Mass.: Community Learning Center, 1973.

Presents basic methods to help the teacher use language experience and integrate it into an on-going adult reading program. Includes the following methods: dictation, transcription, directed writing, and free writing.

Learning Laboratories for Unemployed, Out-of-School Youth: Health Education Part 2. Albany: New York State Department of Education, Bureau of Continuing Education Curriculum Development, 1972.

The learning activities suggested in this publication supplement those found in the curriculum resources handbook "Learning Laboratories for Unemployed, Out-of-School Youth." It deals on a practical level with various health problems in short, achievable units.

Modifying English as a Second Language: Materials for Instructing ABE Students. Albany: New York State Department of Education and SUNY, 1974.

This manual is designed to assist teachers of adult education to modify commercially available ESL materials.

Morrison, Marshall Lee. *A Handbook for Adult Basic Education*. Volume 1. Montgomery: Alabama State Department of Education, n.d.

The general information provided in the handbook is designed to assist adult basic education personnel in planning a program to meet the diverse educational needs of adults.

Patrenella, Luke. *The Newspaper: Food for Thought at the Breakfast Table and in the Classroom of Adult Education*. Austin: Texas Education Agency, Division of Adult and Continuing Education, 1973.

A comprehensive guide on using a newspaper to teach adults in adult and continuing education progress. This publication is a direct result of a newspaper-in-the-classroom production workshop.

Parker, James T. *Competency-Based Adult Education Profile and Related Resources*. Washington, D.C.: Division of Adult Education, U.S. Office of Education, 1976.

This is a listing and a brief description of Adult Performance Level and Competency-Based Adult Education programs currently funded by the states from monies originating in the Division of Adult Education. Included in the second section are resources for priority setting, testing, and curriculum development in APL competency-based adult education programs with information on where they may be obtained, for whom they are appropriate, and how much they cost.

Project Apple Core: Annual Report, July 1, 1975–September 30, 1975. Baton Rouge: Louisiana State Department of Education, 1975.

Staff-initiated instructional programs for people in a variety of local work settings. PIC (Prescriptive Index Card) system provides lists suggesting career-related exercises for basic math skills as well as APL-recommended skills.

Project Communilink: Terminal Report. Ft. Collins: Colorado State University, Department of Education, 1973.

A simulation game, "Microville," was used as a training technique to help develop facilitator/liaison people to be able to plan and implement communitywide adult education and community-improvement programs.

Smith, Robin, and Kozacik, Mary. *Using the Newspaper as an ABE Instructional Aid*. Moline, Ill.: Black Hawk College, 1975.
Materials were developed by a study of newspaper utilization. Contains 48 instructional units.

Suchman, J. Richard, and DiSapio, Martha E. *An Instructional System for Consumer Decision Making*. Teacher's Manual. Carmel, Calif.: Human Resources Research Organization, n.d.
An instructional system is presented for building the competencies of ABE students in making consumer decisions. It offers a guide to teachers who wish to design their own decision-making problems for students.

Wurman, Richard Sail. *Yellow Pages of Learning Resources*. Cambridge, Mass.: The MIT Press, 1972.
A descriptive guide to the people, places, and processes available as learning resources in the urban environment. Sample topics are: "What can you learn from a locksmith?" "What can you learn at a construction site?" "What can you learn about voting?"

2E. BIBLIOGRAPHIES OF CURRICULUM MATERIALS

An Annotated Bibliography of Adult Basic Education and Related Library Materials. Austin: University of Texas, Extension Teaching and Field Service Bureau, 1972.
This is intended as a guide for educators and librarians to select suitable reading materials for adults reading on the first and second grade level. However, the material it cites is mostly for those reading at the sixth grade level and above. Each entry gives a full bibliographic citation, reading level, annotation, and an evaluation.

American Bar Association Clearinghouse for Offender Literacy Progress. *A Reading Program Resource Manual for Adult Basic Education*. Washington, D.C.:, 1974.
Provides information about more than 80 reading programs and systems issued by 40 publishers. Compiled expressly for ABE teachers. Each entry is broken down by publisher, title, scope, purpose, entry level, readability, population for which it was designed, format, record-keeping, remediation, supervision, time to complete, validation, and cost.

Askov, Eunice N., and Lee, Joyce. *An Annotated Bibliography of Adult Basic Education Instructional Materials*. State College Pa.: Pennsylvania State University, College of Education, 1974.

Materials are classified in the following categories: communication skills, life-coping skills, and testing.

Basner, Shari, Boulmetis, John, and Verdi, Marie. *A Curriculum Guide for Adult Educators Based on the Adult Performance Level Study.* Kingston: University of Rhode Island, 1976.
Contains brief descriptions of APL and its objectives. Includes a bibliography for APL content areas. The bibliographic materials are available from companies, employment agencies, the armed services, and counseling services. Reading levels are indicated for each entry.

Bayley, Linda, comp., et al. *ABE: Guide to Library Materials.* Austin: University of Texas, Division of Extension, 1975.
For educators and librarians. Suggests techniques for selecting and displaying materials. Includes annotated bibliography of materials suitable for adult learners.

Berenson, Gail, ed. *A Bibliography of Instructional and Professional Materials for Adult Basic Education.* Portland, Me.: Urban Adult Learning Center, 1977.
A bibliography for ABE teachers and administrators that classifies materials according to content area. Reading levels are indicated for each item.

Cotner, Susan. *Leisure Reading Selection Guide for Public Library and Adult Education Programs, Readability Levels, Annotations, Physical Format, Source, Cost.* Morehead, Ky.: Morehead State University, Appalachian Adult Education Center, 1973.
This was developed with the purpose of providing adults interest themes, easy-to-read materials that adults can use and enjoy.

Gotsick, Priscilla; Moore, Sharon; Cotner, Susan; and Flanery, Joan, comps. *Information for Everyday Survival: What You Need and How to Get It.* Chicago: American Library Association, 1976.
The list was developed at the Appalachian Adult Education Center at Morehead State University, Morehead, Ky. All of the materials are related to problems of everyday life, getting and keeping a job, maintaining a home, caring for children, keeping healthy, managing money, getting along with people, coping with growing older. Each entry is classified by subject; a brief notation describes both the emphasis and the format of the publication. Reading level and approximate cost are noted. Audio-visuals are also included. We found this to be the most comprehensive and easiest to use of all the bibliographies we examined.

Feldman, Marjorie. *Easy Reading Materials for Adults Learning English.* 1976–77 Revised Edition. Chicago: Central YMCA Community College, 1976.
This is divided into the following sections: leisure reading; con-

sumer information; current events, politics in the United States; health, nutrition and family; history and biography, contemporary biographies; and science. Vocabulary level is indicated for some titles.

Johnson, Bill, ed. *Adult Basic Education Instructional Materials Guide*. Ankeny, Iowa: Des Moines Area Community College, 1976.
Provides descriptions of commercial ABE, GED, and ESL materials in the areas of reading, language, and mathematics.

Literacy Volunteers of America, Inc. *1976 Bibliography of Reading Materials for Basic Reading and English as a Second Language*. Syracuse, N.Y.: LVA, 1976.
Prepared for use by volunteer tutors in member organizations of LVA. Student materials are arranged according to reading levels. Publisher and price are also indicated.

Operation Upgrade: A Bibliography of Materials for Adult Education New Readers and Tutors of Adult New Readers. Baton Rouge, La.: Operation Upgrade, 1974.
Contains both Laubach materials and books and workbooks from other publishers that combine reading practice and learning about everyday experiences.

Smith, Jo, and Walden, Bobbie L. *Learning Information for Effective Living: Reading Modules Based on Adult Performance Level Studies*. Consumer Economics—Community Resources. Bulletin No. 18. Montgomery: Alabama State Department of Education, Division of Adult Basic Education, 1976.
Written to provide the adult basic education teacher with practical low-level reading materials on the APL goals and objectives.

Zinn, Lorraine. *A Supplementary Bibliography of Literature Pertaining to Adult Basic Education Staff Development*. Kansas City: Center for Resource Development in Adult Education, School of Education, University of Missouri, 1976.
Contains 122 bibliographic listings directed to the needs of adult educators and teacher-trainers. All references are available from ERIC.

2F. THE USE OF BROADCAST MEDIA

Adult Literacy: Progress in 1975/76. London: Her Majesty's Stationery Office, 1976.
A report on the first year's operation of the Adult Literacy Resource Agency's management committee, and on its work to support the BBC's literacy program by recruiting and training

volunteer tutors. Over 45,000 tutors were recruited, almost 36,000 trained, and 55,000 students had begun learning to read.

BBC Adult Literacy Handbook. London: British Broadcasting Corporation, 1975. Revised edition, 1977.

A tutors' guide designed to accompany the BBC Adult Literacy Project, which began in October 1975. It provides advice to those teaching adult illiterates as well as those organizing programs. The first section analyzes what the authors' evidence about the causes of adult illiteracy and the kinds of skills tutors need. The second section offers a variety of specific suggestions for teaching adults with different kinds of reading problems. The final section examines the difficulties faced by organizers of literacy programs.

BBC Adult Literacy Project: Post-publication Mini-Research Project on "Your Move." University of Reading (England), Department of Typography and Graphic Communication, 1977.

An evaluation of the effectiveness of some of the graphic conventions used in *Your Move*, a program of the BBC's literacy project.

Burke, Richard C. *The Use of Radio in Adult Literacy Education*. Tehran: Hulton Educational Publications Ltd., in cooperation with the International Institute for Adult Literacy Methods, 1976.

Provides specific and down-to-earth advice to field workers in developing countries about using radio broadcasting as a tool in literacy education. Includes brief annotated bibliography and list of organizations that might provide additional information. One of a series of training monographs on literacy in development.

Descriptive Overview of a Technology-Based Open Learning System: The GED Project at Kentucky Educational Television. Lexington: Kentucky Educational Television, n.d.

Overview of an educational television series produced in Kentucky and aimed at adults preparing for the GED examination (high school equivalency diploma). Programs in the series covered such topics as English grammar, mathematics, and reading; teachers' guides to these programs are published by and available from Cambridge Book Company, New York.

Devereux, W. A. "The Adult Literacy Campaign in the United Kingdom." In *Convergence*, Vol. 10, No. 1, 1977.

An article based on Devereux's report on the Adult Literacy Resource Agency's first year of operation in the United Kingdom. Provides a historical overview of work to increase public awareness of the extent of illiteracy in Britain; to increase the cadre of professional and volunteer staff; to reduce the stigma of illiteracy; and to set up a network of public and private agencies to deal with the educational needs of adult learners who come forward as a result of the BBC campaign.

A Handbook for ETV Utilization in Adult Education. Final Report. Vol. 3, 1975. Morehead, Ky.: Appalachian Adult Education Center, Morehead State University, 1975.

This is a handbook for administration of adult education programs. It is based upon a study conducted in Kentucky of an educational television series aimed at adults preparing for the GED exam (high school equivalency diploma). The handbook discusses ETV in terms of five major components—planning and management, promotion and recruitment, manpower development, materials and curricula, and student needs and intake systems—and includes PERT charts and diagrams of the delivery system.

Hargreaves, David. *On the Move: The BBC's Contribution to the Adult Literacy Campaign in the United Kingdom between 1972 and 1976*. London: BBC Education, Summer 1977.

A personal account by the project leader of the BBC's adult literacy program, describing the history of the BBC's contribution to the British adult literacy campaign.

Just Around the Corner: Student Book, Series 1. New York: Cambridge Book Co., 1977.

The student workbook for *Just Around the Corner*, an adult education series produced for the Mississippi Authority for Educational TV. A number of supplementary pamphlets, a teachers' guide, and a prospectus for the series are published by and available from the Mississippi Authority for Educational TV.

Korf, Michele J. *Feasibility Study: Fundamental Adult Education Services and the Role of Instructional Television*. Report prepared for Educational Broadcasting Corporation, WNET/13. New York: WNET/13, unpublished, 1976.

An evaluation of the feasibility of using broadcast media in fundamental adult education. The study was initiated in response to the situation created by cutbacks in funding for educationally disadvantaged adults in New York City. It concludes that more research is needed but suggests that if electronic media were successfully related to schools, work situations and other institutions, they could, perhaps, in the long run provide the most cost-effective means of meeting growing educational needs.

MacFarlane, Tom. *Teaching Adults to Read*. London: Adult Literacy Resource Agency, 1976.

Describes a practical working method of helping adults with reading, writing, and spelling difficulties, using content of interest to the learner. This is one of a series of booklets published by ALRA, which has since completed its mandate to provide support to the BBC literacy project. Inquiries may be addressed to Interprint Graphic Services Ltd., Half Moon Street, Bagshot, Surrey, England. Others in the series are *An Approach to Functional Literacy, Training in Adult Literacy Schemes*, and *Resource Pack for Volunteer Tutors*.

Maddison, John. *Radio and Television in Literacy*. Paris: UNESCO, 1971.

Part of UNESCO's "Reports and Papers on Mass Communication" series. Maddison describes the use of broadcast media to combat adult illiteracy in the Third World and in the U.S.; discusses methods and materials, concepts of literacy and feedback; and concludes that all ways of using broadcast media should be explored by countries with high illiteracy rates, and that such use of the media should be part of overall development of new social, economic, and educational communications techniques.

Open Education for the People. A Report by the Educational Broadcasting Corporation to the City of New York on the Use of Broadcasting to Maximize Educational Opportunity. New York: Educational Broadcasting Corporation, April 1976.

This report is divided into five sections: Part 1, the role of broadcast media to help meet publicly identified educational needs; Part 2, discussion of the educational/broadcasting partnership necessary to meet educational needs; Part 3, discussion of WNYC-FM radio; Part 4, conclusions and recommendations for planning, development, and implementation; and Part 5, references and notes.

Public Broadcasting and Education: Report of the Task Force on Adult Education. Advisory Council of National Organizations to the Corporation for Public Broadcasting. Washington, D.C.: Corporation for Public Broadcasting, 1975.

A set of general recommendations for priorities in coordination in the CPB with reference, first, to adult basic education and vocational/technical education. Subgroups working on recommendations in specific areas saw television broadcast as a means of supplementing ongoing programs like ABE, but outlined no specific steps for the realization of this objective.

Stevens, Jenny. "The BBC Adult Literacy Project." In *Convergence*, Vol. 10, No. 1, 1977.

A description of the BBC's role in the adult literacy campaign in the United Kingdom. The development of the broadcast elements of the program is described—including the process of testing and feedback. The referral support service, the study materials, promotion and publicity, training of volunteers, and future plans are all detailed, thus providing the reader an overview of the intricate, interdependent network that grew around the BBC effort.

Training in Adult Literacy Schemes. London: Adult Literacy Resources Agency, n.d.

A brief guide for organizers of literacy programs that will be using volunteer tutors, based on experience in training 40,000 volunteers for the British literacy campaign.

Index

NOTE: Page numbers in italic indicate tables or figures.